BRANDTASTIC OR BRAND TERRIBLE?

SARAH BRUMMITT

www.sarahbrummitt.com

Brandtastic or Brand Terrible?

ISBN 978-184426-419-3

First Published 2007 by
BEST FOOT FORWARD PRESS
An Imprint of Upfront Publishing, Peterborough, UK.

www.sarahbrummitt.com

Printed by Printondemand-Worldwide Ltd.

For Sue Harris, a woman with
an extraordinary personal brand.

Sarah Brummitt

Introduction

'There is only one thing in the world worse than being talked about, and that is not being talked about.'

Oscar Wilde, *The Picture of Dorian Gray, 1891*

What do others say when they talk about you? 'Creative'? 'Professional'? 'Reliable'? Or perhaps 'scruffy'? 'Dull'? 'Always late'? What they're referring to is your personal brand. This thing you've been building up throughout the course of your career to date. Much like any commercial brand, it may have strengths or weaknesses associated with it. The truth is that you most certainly have one. This book will help you explore yours.

The area of personal branding is huge so let me begin by managing your expectations. My focus will be what I call the 'shop window' – your image and personal impact. There's plenty more to personal branding than what we'll cover here – and that's deliberate. When working with professionals, the most common theme I hear in response to questions about their reading material is that yes, they've all got plenty of interesting books, journals and articles awaiting their attention. What's missing is time – there just isn't enough of it to get through the books or journals at home or in the office. You can read this book on a plane or even in a couple of days commuting on a train. Again, that's intentional. It's a taster for those of you who've never even considered what your personal brand is – let alone tried proactively to build it to get what you want from your career – but there's enough here to get you thinking about new ideas and new approaches and certainly enough for you to take action.

Before we get into the detail a word of warning. Personal branding is *not* about style over substance. No matter your profession, if you don't have the skills, technical capabilities and attitude to support your image then you will find it very tough to get what you want from your career. However, the flip side of this coin is also true. You may have all of the talent in the world, but if you also have a poorly managed image then you will have certainly lost out on some great career, sales or leadership opportunities in the past. And you might not even realise what they were. But you knew that, right? That's why you've picked up this book. Be open-minded to the possibility that you can make some changes. Take what you need from this book and ignore the rest. But most importantly try some different things as a result of what you've read here. What you know isn't as interesting as what you *do* with what you know.

Experiment and see what happens. If it doesn't work – simply change it and try something else.

Enjoy the book.

Sarah Brummitt

Contents

Chapter Three : Walking the Talk

Chapter Four : Behaviour That's Bad News

Chapter Five : Language and Personal Branding

Sarah Brummitt

BRANDTASTIC

OR BRAND TERRIBLE?

Sarah Brummitt

Chapter One
Introduction to Personal Branding and Image

The What, How and Why of This Book

The purpose of this book is to help you understand the business value of your image and personal impact, as part of 'Brand You'. Think about how much time, effort and money has been spent on getting you to where you are in your career at the moment? You represent an expensive investment – are you making the most of it? Are you clear on what you represent professionally? And is everyone else? And are you consistent? Maximising your personal brand is an ongoing activity. It's not just about reading a book or attending a course and then that's it, job done. It's dynamic, evolving, a moving feast.

Secondly, this book is designed to be very practical. I will encourage you to be honest with yourself about what exactly *is* the kind of impact that you currently make? I'll also encourage you to go and ask others – people you work with and people you trust.

The point is not to evoke crises of confidence or tears before bedtime, but rather to do what a lot of people claim they do regularly – seek honest, constructive feedback which is positively intended and easily implemented.

How To Use This Book

You can – as is fairly common with reading books – start at the beginning and keep going, either in one hit or on a chapter-by-chapter basis. I shall review some of the research and data presented by some of the leading experts in this area. Alternatively, you can dip in and out of the book by sections. Periodically throughout the book, I have provided you with a space to reflect and think about what you've learned but – more importantly – plan what you can do with what you've learned. It's your choice.

Why You Should Carry On Reading

My intent is that this book will enable you to do a number of important things in relation to your personal brand; you will be able to:

(i)   Define your personal brand. What is it now? And what ideally do you want it to be?

(ii) Understand how to reinforce your brand through your personal presentation, non-verbal and verbal language.

(iii) Gain practical knowledge and skills to enable you to influence others perceptions of you in a positive way

(iv) Increase your self awareness and self confidence

(v)   Improve your personal effectiveness. How come? By being more aware of your brand; you can make intentional choices about how to leverage it to your advantage with colleagues, customers and the wider business community in which you operate. You're in charge of your personal brand now; rather than it being in charge of you.

Never Judge A Book By Its Cover: The Personal Branding Phenomenon

Think about your day so far – you woke up (at home; or maybe in a hotel) to the sound of the radio; perhaps the television or the hotel alarm call (with its immediate message about the hotel/facilities/special rates and demands to have a nice day when you're barely conscious.) You shower and dress, using a range of toiletries, hair products and cosmetics. (I'll go out on a limb here and assume the last item is directed largely at female readers). You get dressed, wearing clothes which comprise your favourite casual outfit or maybe a work suit, gather up your phone, keys, briefcase, handbag or man bag – I'm gender neutral, seriously – and head for breakfast. You can see where I'm going here. You pick up your preferred newspaper that's been delivered to your home (or room), gather up the post which comprises a range of bills, catalogues, fliers etc and sit down to eat and read. I haven't even mentioned the consumer brands that abound at the breakfast table. The point is simply this: you're bombarded with brand messages constantly. Imagine how many brands you've been exposed to during the day if you're reading this book at eight o'clock at night.

What Do We Mean By The Term 'Brands'?

Quite simply brands are relationships. In commercial terms, a brand is how your customers, suppliers, business partners and the like describe what their experience is of doing business with you. The fact is simply this: it's their definition of what it's like to have a business relationship with you – rather than yours. Any organisation will tell you that they have a great brand – but whilst this is absolutely true for certain organisations, it is wishful thinking for many, many others.

A great example of the power of brands is the Gerald Ratner story. Ratner used to be a nationwide chain of jewellers and a familiar face on the UK high street, positioned as a jeweller offering discounted products. However, in an extraordinary, career-terminating move by Ratner himself, he joked during a 1991 speech to the Institute of Directors that one of his firm's products was 'total crap', and boasted that some of its earrings were 'cheaper than an M&S prawn sandwich'. Oh dear. No one found it that funny and shareholders at Ratner certainly weren't laughing when they realised that the speech had been recorded and instantly reported across the media. How bad did it get? Catastrophic is the short answer. The damage to the brand was irrevocable. 'Ratners' equalled 'crap jewellery' and who would want to be associated with that? In financial terms an estimated £500m was wiped off the value of the company, the man himself departed the following year and the name 'Ratner' was removed altogether from the business in 1994.

As an aside, (bear with me, I may have a few of these), our sense of humour is unquestionably part of the package that makes up our personal brand. The Gerald Ratner saga is a salutary lesson in the gap between how funny we think we are and how funny others actually find us. Your ability to be funny, much like your brand, is determined by the experience others have of you and your humour – it's their view that counts, not your own. The golden rule is this: if you have to explain that you were being funny, or that your comments were only a joke, then believe me, you *weren't* funny. Gerald Ratner found that out to his considerable cost.

What Is A Personal Brand?

A personal brand simply takes the same principle of brands in business and applies it to you as an individual. It is how others would describe the experience of having a professional relationship with you. Are you smart? Creative? Dynamic? Impressive? Inspirational? Or are you lax? Unreliable? Unassertive? Aggressive? Or ineffectual? An absolutely critical point to make about brands is the 'c' word – consistency. If you are professional, creative and dynamic on some days (but frankly you're boring, rude, patronising or disinterested on others), then your brand isn't likely to be widely recognised in the terms you want. You have to be consistent in order to build the brand you want.

Take a moment to think of two people with whom you currently work: one you 'rate' and one you don't. How would you describe them? What are the adjectives that come to mind? What you're describing is your brand perception of them. This could be as a result of working with them over time or based on only one or two interactions. The point is that you have brand relationships with both of them.

Is it possible not to have a brand? 'No' is the simple answer. You've got a brand, even if you're the most quiet, introverted, 'non-existent' person in the office. By the way, that's your brand which I've just described. You've definitely got one. Now you know, and it leads nicely to a very interesting point raised by the experts who've written about personal branding at length. Quite simply, vast swathes of the professional community are branded *accidentally*. They have no idea that they've been developing a brand over time, so they fail to make the most of their strengths and continue to be hi-jacked by their weaknesses. Remember, it's impossible not to have a brand! The point of this book is to help build your brand intentionally by looking at your image and personal impact.

The Shop Window Versus The Goods Displayed Inside

Imagine yourself as a shop window. Work with me here. How you appear and behave could cause people who meet you for the first time to think:

(i)   He looks good
(ii)   She looks and behaves in an impressive way
(iii)   That's someone I want to know more about
(iv)   That's a scruffy person
(v)   That's a nice guy but not impressive
(vi)   What a buffoon!
(vii) And any number of other *first impressions*.

A question I'm often asked relates to the notion of whether or not personal brand is the same as our actual personality, personal beliefs, traits and so on. Let's be clear. Your personal brand is *not* a reflection of you as an entire human being. Don't get confused. If we're talking about maximising your personal brand through your image and personal impact then we're talking about effectively managing the enduring perception that others have of you. That's quite a different thing.

What Can A Great Personal Brand Do For You?

No doubt this is a valid question. Remember, I've already said that personal brands aren't about style over substance. So why might you even want to build, manage or maintain a great personal brand? Experts in this field will argue that certainly a great personal brand enables you to stand out from the crowd. This notion of being the first name that comes to mind can enable you to have a head start on new career, sales or leadership opportunities.

Interested but not yet convinced? Well consider some other potential benefits. Having a great personal brand is attractive. People want to work with you, have your involvement, glean your opinions, learn from you, respect what you say and be part of your team. This almost goes back to those long-lost days at school when you suffered the experience in PE of being picked for school sports teams. No matter how poor your hand-eye co-ordination was during those formative years, don't tell me that you didn't want to be picked by the cool, attractive hockey/football/ netball captain, rather than skulking around, trying not to look bothered, disappointed and crushed with rejection alongside all the other real losers.

A great personal brand gets you noticed and gets you recognition. You can earn more, get promoted and have your ideas and suggestions adopted – all because of being in this 'stand out from the crowd' position.

What Can't A Great Personal Brand Do For You?

It can't hide incompetence. Let's not kid ourselves here – we all know or have met people in business about whom we think, 'How the hell did they manage to get to that position?' Maybe that's luck, or maybe it's our perception and they're actually quite good at exactly what the organisation needs them to be – as opposed to what we'd like them to be. Either way, a great personal brand *won't* cover up a lack of technical ability in the long run. If you're not good enough you will be found out and your colleagues' brand perception of you will change to reflect that fact.

Great personal brands can't hide the fact that you have to work hard, be clear on your goal, stay focused and learn from you mistakes. Another aside – if you were just thinking, having read the previous sentence, that, 'I don't make mistakes,' then *wrong*!! You do, you have and you don't realise it. Worse, you're not learning from them if you don't admit the possibility that you might not be perfect, then you're bound, therefore, to repeat them. Wake up and be realistic.

Being Caught By An Attractive Shop Window

Which elements of your 'shop window' are most significant when meeting someone for the first time, would you say?

Take a moment to really consider this question. If you wish, make a note below.

In terms of your shop window, there's a lot of research in business about *how* we form these initial impressions. We do this based on what we see, not what we hear in the first instance. The 'seeing' aspect incorporates appearance and non-verbal communication. Irrespective of how politically correct we are, it's impossible *not* to form impressions of others when we meet them – *especially* for the first time. Given that this is true, the question then becomes 'how quickly?' There's some interesting Canadian research into web pages which identified how long it takes before we register an impression as to their visual appeal. Believe it or not, the research noted that it can be as quickly as 50 milliseconds. Literally in the blink of an eye, we make what are nearly instantaneous judgments. As far as forming impressions of humans as opposed to web sites goes, much of your image is projected within 30 seconds, although there's some data to suggest our first impression is formed even more quickly than this.

Misquoting Mehrabian

Here's an important but momentary aside (I did warn you). Professor Albert Mehrabian's work is often misquoted and misunderstood in the whole area of non-verbal communication. You may well have come across statistics which regale the proportion of what we do that influences the message we communicate. Figures of 55% for body language, 38% for voice and 7% for verbal language are regularly banded about. Actually this isn't right.

Nonverbal communication describes Mehrabian's research. He constructed a number of inconsistent messages about feelings. Each message included three specific components: specific words, specific vocal qualities, and specific facial expressions. Each component was designed to convey a specific attitude (positive or negative) and a specific strength (e.g. strong liking or mild disliking). Mehrabian constructed inconsistent messages by combining components of differing strengths and attitudes.

Mehrabian observed people giving and receiving these mixed messages, and assessed the receiver's perception of the sender's feeling. From this information, Mehrabian performed a linear regression to assess the extent to which each component contributed to the receiver's perception of the sender's feeling. That's where the percentages come from and we have to be very careful about what we infer from the statistics. However, having said all that, for the purposes of being technically accurate, putting forward the idea that a lot of what we communicate comes across in our body language is certainly a reasonable suggestion.

There has been some interesting research conducted by my colleagues in the image profession which found that when it comes to the interview process, the second most important criterion was personal presentation and it was more highly ranked than having an MBA. Previous experience or technical capability didn't top the list, communication skills did.

In addition, a wider cross section of business professionals were also surveyed and it was found that 80% of them form impressions on how well a colleague can do his or her job by their clothing and grooming. So – whether we like it or not – we will be judged – now and in the future – on the visual first impressions.

The UK Conservative Party leadership election in 2005 was an interesting example of the impact of image. Initially it was an open-and-shut case when Michael Howard resigned back in May 2005 after the General Election defeat. David Davis was the front-runner by a country mile, right up to the Conservative Party Conference in October 2005. When you looked at David Cameron, leaving aside for a moment whether or not you agree with his policies, the image that he projected throughout the conference aligned very much with the direction the Conservative Party and its members wanted to go in: fresh, modern, smart, dynamic, authoritative and forward-thinking. His presentation to the conference delegates – delivered without notes or autocue – was a triumph. It all added up to a very persuasive personal impact and as a result, he won the leadership election in convincing fashion.

Pause For Thought

- What have you learned from the material you've read so far?

- What are the key insights to note?

- Are there any actions you should take as a result of this learning? You can note them on the personal brand action plan at the back of this book or put them somewhere you will definitely be prompted to actually do them.

Do Corporate And Individual Brands Add Up?

If you can accept that image and personal impact is important to your 'shop window' (and trust me, it is), now let's bring in the notion of brands. If organisations are to survive, they design, develop and deliver great products and services to their customers which their customers not only value but are also prepared to pay for. If you were to ask the managing director or CEO of any organisation what's going to help differentiate their business from their competitors, you'll hear the answer 'our people' appear very quickly. It strikes me as very odd that businesses invest heavily in their corporate identity and 'personality on the web' (otherwise known to you and me as a website). They go on and on and on about their brand.

15

But what about the brand of an organisation's employees? If we believe that people are at the heart of an organisation's culture, and ultimately success, and that brands are central to differentiating companies from their competitors, then what about joining the two together? What about the brand of the individuals within an organisation? Individuals within any organisation should reflect some of the corporate values, shouldn't they? I recently went to Bangkok and flew on Thai Airways for the first time. Not only are all the staff (particularly the women) immaculately attired, but they actually change their uniform completely during the flight, so they appear in two very smart, colour-coordinated, fitted outfits. That's how much importance Thai Airways puts behind projecting its brand values through the image of its staff.

The Most Influential Parts Of Your 'Shop Window'

Your shop window is a metaphor for your personal brand. Every great personal brand has three to five attributes that are very clear to anyone who comes in to contact with that brand. Typically your shop window is made up of your:

(i) Personal image: By this I mean your clothing and accessories plus your personal grooming.

(ii) Non-verbal behaviour: By this I mean how you behave. Initially, the kinds of things that are noticed particularly are your handshake, eye contact, facial expression, your posture and your gestures.

(iii) Verbal Behaviour: By this I mean the speed at which you speak, your verbal tone and variation, your diction, and any 'rubbish words' (by that I mean words or phrases which add absolutely nothing to what you're saying and have no place in the sentence at all). By the way, I've deliberately left out the content of what you say because this tends *initially* to be less important.

What Is Your Personal Brand?

When I pose this question to my clients, sometimes I may hear characteristics, rather than brand values. What I mean by this is information which is technically true (working mother, business studies graduate, catholic, Chelsea supporter etc.). Although this is interesting, it's not actually relevant to your brand because this is a *characteristic* of you or a 'feature' in sales terminology. Brands may have many, many characteristics. Personal brand values are all about benefits, so you need to think of words or phrases that describe the *benefits* of working with you. Think of ones that are relevant, believable and distinctive. Just thought I'd mention that before posing the following questions. Make a note overleaf if you need to.

What are the attributes or adjectives that represent the core essence of you? What are your personal brand values - your sense of how you want to be perceived by colleagues, friends, family and the wider world? Remember, you should write down words that reflect *relevant* brand values for the job that you do, and are comfortable to use to describe the essence of you.

Personal Brands in Action

Who do you know personally that has a great brand? Now, ask yourself, 'Why'? What is it about them that makes you think the way you do?

Are these the kinds of adjectives you would want others to say about you? They don't have to be. The point is simply this – you are aiming to have others (whose point of view you care about), readily describe you in the terms you would *most like*. That's the goal of not just identifying your personal brand through these adjectives, but also the result of any action you subsequently take.

Beginning The Journey

Believe it or not, you've already started working on evolving the brand *you* want. You now have your ideal or desired 'personal brand adjectives'.

However, it makes sense to find out for certain where you are *now*. Identify at least three people who you believe have the capacity to be honest. Don't necessarily go to those closest to you (they don't want to hurt feelings and it's easier for them to lie – trust me). The purpose of this exercise is honest reflection, not unwarranted narcissism. Ask them what their brand perception of you is – the good, the bad and the ugly – and explore what the basis is for their perception by providing specific examples. This exercise means that it's not a love-fest with your three closest pals. You need a balanced, honest view, not one from behind rose-tinted glasses.

The Rules of Feedback

This could be classed as an aside – but I'm going to make it anyway. (I did warn you there would be a few of these). As an executive coach, I spend a lot of my working life coaching and giving feedback. It's amazing to me how often I find professionals who say they welcome feedback but act in a way which appears to completely contradict that assertion when feedback is shared. (Obviously I'm speaking about developmental feedback primarily). Indeed, in my career to date I've worked with individuals who behave as if they're perfect. (If only!) Back to my point. In the process of asking for feedback about your brand, be prepared to hear some things that may surprise you and which may not be the most flattering. Here are the rules for just such a situation:

Do	*Don't*
Encourage absolute honesty.	Dismiss anything shared by those who give you feedback. Remember brands are about others' perceptions of you. If one person thinks that; others could and probably do.
Listen fully (rather than waiting to jump in at the first opportunity to explain yourself).	Discount their opinion – deciding that you don't much like, respect or care for them anyway.
Make notes.	Get frustrated.
Ask questions.	Take it personally.
Get specific examples.	Rationalise your behaviour (e.g. 'there was a good reason I was rude/late/dull that day' and so on).
Explore how you can project your brand more positively.	Be pig-headed and resolutely refuse to change anything.

Remember, even if you don't agree with their opinion you can't invalidate it. And, part of the reason for reading this book is, I hope, to make choices about your image and personal impact which will positively influence others' brand perception of you.

And One More Thing Before They Get Stuck In With Their Comments...

When I talk about asking your colleagues to be specific what may help is some context setting. You are about to make an unusual request, so don't hesitate to remind them that:

(i)   Positive intent is also the name of the game here. Anything shared must come from this place, because we're asking for feedback to enhance our image and personal brand still further – not destroy us and undermine our sense of ourselves.

(ii) Confidentiality is king. The information shared between you must remain between you – and is not for debate over lunch with others or at a later stage with colleagues.

(iii) Specificity rather than vague generalisations are required here. Ask your colleagues to avoid language such as 'always', 'never', 'everyone' or 'no one'.

(iv) Objectivity and specificity are needed. For example, 'I wouldn't wear that top because it makes you look like a tart', or 'You look like a moron in that shirt,' isn't as helpful as, 'That top shows a lot of your cleavage when you lean forward,' or 'That shirt's pattern and colour makes you look pale and large around the belly.' That allows you to make the choice about whether or not wearing said top/shirt would be a good idea in the future.

(v) Privacy for the conversation is also important. Go somewhere where you have space to think and talk openly – which rules out the tube, the canteen, the middle of the office and the lavatory.

Don't forget to capture their comments and make your own notes in the personal brand feedback audit at the back of this book.

Time For Honesty With Yourself

Now that you've had an honest conversation with your colleagues, it's time for some authentic reflection of your own about your personal brand. What works? What doesn't? What are you really communicating about your values through your image and personal impact? What are you saying that you *really* don't want to say? Make a note of your own observations alongside those of your colleagues on your personal brand feedback audit.

Now That I've Got All This Feedback, What Do I Do With It?

You should now have some (hopefully) objective feedback on your current brand. What have you learned? Were there any surprises? What does the feedback say about how effectively you are *currently* aligning your brand through your image?

Take stock of your feedback and personal reflection and identify:

(i)   Your key insights

(ii) The key areas from this book that you now need to understand in more detail

Joining Up The Dots

You now have feedback on your current brand and you have identified what you want to focus on to hone your personal brand. An interesting question for you to consider as we move into the next section of this book is this: what does the feedback you've received say about how effectively you are *currently* aligning your brand and that of your company through your image? For example, take the term 'professional'. What does that mean in terms of your brand? Although you may not have automatically identified a personal brand value of 'quality', I'm struggling to think that you *wouldn't* want to be known as representing that brand value as a professional. This doesn't mean all designer labels and logos. Some people can look positively ghastly in designer clothes. How quality is represented and communicated through your clothing is by well-cut, well-fitting, clean, pressed clothes which are the right colour, combined with quality accessories and immaculate grooming.

Chapter Two
Key Image Issues

The Power Of Six

Managing your image to look good consistently means understanding what I call the 'power of six' - six factors which affect the impact and visual appeal of your appearance. We'll take a look at each in some detail but believe me, if you adhere to these principles you'll never again have a day when someone else thinks you got dressed in the dark.

(i) Appropriate

What a great word. It's one of those words which, whilst we all know what it literally means, we may have absolutely no idea about how to interpret it – or at least, how to do so consistently across a wide range of situations! So, let me be clear. When I use the word 'appropriate' what I specifically mean is three things:

(i)   What you are doing?

(ii) Where you are doing it?

(iii) When you are doing it?

Let's take the first sub-category for a moment: the situation. Are you going for an interview? Are you running a team meeting? Are you delivering an important presentation? Hosting a conference call? In other words what is the activity you'll be involved in?

Where you are doing it means simply the environment. Are you at your company's global head offices? A client's office? A hotel? There are also some more subtle considerations to note. Are you indoors or outside for example? Is it a hot climate or a cold climate? All of these sorts of issues link to the notion of considering others. By that I mean unless you're on your own with absolutely no one else around, (unlikely, I'm sure you'd agree), what are others around you wearing? And what, given the environment, is their expectation of what you should wear?

When you are doing it is all about time of day, obviously. What time of day is it? Is it a day time, or evening event?

You see, there's more to this 'appropriate' lark than you might at first think.

Dress Code Or Dress Confusion?

My research in preparation for this book revealed one thing very clearly. Every image professional I have talked to seems to have a different view regarding 'dress codes' and what is deemed 'correct' attire for both business and social situations. Excellent news, glad I asked. Perhaps that's why everyone is so confused. To add further irony to the situation, I just thought I would share some real life examples of dress codes that have come my way. Here's hoping you will never have to face up to any of these:

(i) Mediterranean Business Attire. Seriously. This was for a sales conference in Cyprus which I attended.

(ii) Ethically Responsible Clothing with Style. Another beauty I came across for a wedding reception. I didn't go because I love leather handbags and shoes. What can I say? I didn't want to upset the bride or groom on their big day, and I certainly was not going attend accessorised to the hilt in plastic.

(iii) 'Con Brio'. For a party attended by my husband's cousin and his wife. It's almost as if the hosts were not content with creating a whole new code, they thought it would be fun to spice things up by communicating their style guidelines in a foreign language. How they must have laughed when getting that printed on the invitations. (If you're interested, the gentlemen in question wore a red velvet smoking jacket and looked fabulous).

Hopefully you don't have to wrestle with these sartorial guidelines on a regular basis. If you do, contact me – you can't possibly have the time to deal with this sort of nonsense and need an image coach to make sense of it all, and quickly. My personal view is that the more information provided around 'dos' and 'don'ts' for each 'code of dress', the better it must be. People need guidance and specifics, not generalisations and guesswork. Let's start at the super-smart, suited and booted end of the scale and work our way back to laid-back, casual attire.

Professional Business Wear

Professional business wear means exactly what it says. The look (or brand image you want to project) is very formal and 'professional'. It's your absolutely most smart look for work. For ladies this translates to a suit (ideally a skirt suit) which is made of a smooth, dark and plain fabric, worn with high-quality shoes and accompanied by a briefcase. Accompanying the suit is a smart, structured work shirt or blouse. Additional accessories such as jewellery are classic, simple and unobtrusive. Personal grooming is sleek and immaculate. Can women wear trouser suits for the professional business dress code? Yes, if they adhere to the principles I've just described. (A momentary aside if I may: some of my clients, and colleagues come to that, get incredibly hung up on whether a skirt suit is seen as being 'smarter' than a trouser suit. There is some research to suggest that a skirt suit is *perceived to be* smarter than a trouser suit, however my personal view is that you need to take in the whole picture.)

In other words the quality of the suit, shirt or blouse worn with the suit, as well as the accessories and jewellery are also key, as is personal grooming, to whether or not someone looks 'super smart' in a suit. And this is a more useful question than the whole skirt/trouser debate. I've seen women look ghastly in skirt suits because the other pieces of the jigsaw weren't right and conversely, I've seen women look amazing in trouser suits. Gentlemen, for you, similar principles apply for the professional business look (assuming, though, you don't wear skirts). A high quality, smooth, plain, dark suit, worn with a crisp, plain white shirt with double cuffs and cufflinks (not naff ones), is at the heart of this look. Naturally you need a tie, with a colour and pattern which are entirely appropriate. Ties for men are a great expression of your personal brand values, so enjoy your choice here, but just beware of the garish or distracting. That's not a brand value you want associated with you (is it?). Shoes should be black, smooth and highly polished; socks should be dark (think of the brand values associated with white socks if you dare), accessories should be high-quality and personal grooming, immaculate.

Relaxed Business Wear

Relaxed business wear is still a professional look, but – hence the name – it has a slightly more relaxed, informal air to it. For ladies what this practically translates to is a number of different things: you could wear an unmatched skirt suit or unmatched trousers with a jacket. A more casual (or lesser quality) trouser suit may also fall into this category. There is likely to be more knitwear or T-shirts in evidence with the jackets and 'bottom halves', and undoubtedly more colour and pattern will also appear. Similarly for gentlemen you can wear more colour and patterns in the suits, and you could also opt for a single-cuff, button-down shirt or a suit without a tie. Shoes and accessories will be more casual (so for example a loafer shoe could be worn) and there is more choice of patterns on the shoes.

Smart Or Business Casual

Unlike its predecessors from the school of dress code, this young filly is the one which causes the most confusion. Smart casual (or business casual – I'll use the terms inter-changeably) is a classic oxymoron. Before I even get to that, the very fact that it has two possible definitions should be our first clue to the reality that most professionals have absolutely no idea what the acceptable norms here are – never mind project their personal brand values effectively through this style of dress. Indeed, when I talk to clients about this definition it's a bit like lighting the fuse to a rocket. I merely stand back and wait for the fireworks. My key thoughts on this style of dressing are as follows: you still need to project a look of quality, even though you are more casually attired. It has to be a look which commands respect, shows attention to detail and reflects immaculate personal grooming, even though it is not as business-like as the previous two styles of dress.

For ladies this means good quality, smart, co-ordinated separates. This means either skirts or trousers; a jacket isn't essential; more casual shoes, bags and accessories – but not cheap looking! Don't think that what you wear to push a trolley around a supermarket will do. It won't. You can certainly wear more knitwear with more texture, colour and pattern. At the risk of repeating myself – but too bad, it's important – quality and co-ordination is key. Invest in smart casual clothing – and I mean invest – rather than think, 'It'll do.' Remember the saying, 'It'll do usually doesn't' when it comes to 'business casual'.

For gentlemen, the same principles apply. Quality pieces which co-ordinate are key to this look. Well-fitting knitwear, smart, well-fitting trousers are in evidence, quality fabrics such as linen, moleskin, needle-cord and cotton abound, shirts without ties are in evidence are as more colours (including browns) and patterns across all items of clothing and footwear. A suede brogue, for example, would fall into this category for gentlemen. Again, a jacket isn't a necessity. When I first completed my initial training as an image consultant I was told that if a man wears brown shoes it definitely means a 'smart casual' look. I wasn't initially convinced; now I am. The difference that *makes* the difference with 'smart casual' is colour and choice of fabric.

The Jeans Jury

I can't leave this standard of dress code alone without talking about jeans. Almost everyone owns at least one pair and it really is a topic that can spark debate! The question is this, can you wear jeans and still project appropriate brand values around quality, respect and an appropriate look for work? Well, it depends. Let me visit the 'f-word' first of all. The jeans have got to fit. If the waistband is half way down your legs or nearly touching your armpits, your jeans don't fit properly. If they have holes or elaborate patterns, are too tight, look too sexy, or are straining at the seams, then they aren't appropriate. If they're dirty, creased or stained, then they aren't appropriate. If you don't wear them with a belt (gentlemen please take particular note here), then they don't look right. If you paid a small fortune for them, don't assume that means they represent good quality or at least, project an image of good quality in the work environment. If they are white, pink or any other sherbet colour then they aren't appropriate for work. Jeans *can* pass muster in the business environment for work *if:*

(i)   They fit correctly and are clean, un-creased, without holes, rips, patches, embroidery or any other adornment.

(ii)   You have paid close attention to what they are worn with. By this I mean two more things. Firstly: quality accessories. So gentlemen, think about a decent belt, smart leather shoes, brogues or loafers etc. Trainers, cowboy boots or biker boots are all absolute non-starters. Ladies, the same goes for you too – and make sure you have a smart, decent handbag or briefcase than a rucksack or more casual fabric bag. Secondly, the other issue is what you wear on the upper half of your body. So for gentlemen, a decent shirt with patterns and colour is absolutely fine, but double cuffs and cufflinks creates an infinitely different more professional look to teaming your jeans with a T-shirt or polo shirt.

Ladies: a crisp white shirt with cuffs and a smart jacket looks very different – and much more professional – than a strappy T-shirt underneath a ballet top and low-slung, boot-cut jeans which reveal your underwear (and a dash more) when you bend down. My verdict as a panellist sitting on the jeans jury is this: many people get jeans wrong at work. That's why it doesn't project a professional look. You can do it – but you must team quality, well-fitting jeans with the right accessories and right choice of clothing on the upper half of your body.

Business Casual Which Isn't Good Enough For Business

Many organisations have migrated to business or smart casual in the last five years. However, guidelines around what is and is not appropriate appear to be thin on the ground. Why is that? Whenever I initiate this whole area of discussion with professionals there is no doubt that everyone has an opinion on what should and should not be worn for work, and we can all relate to instances in which a colleague clearly failed to consider they attire, and preferred to douse themselves in glue and go running through their wardrobes.

My point is simply this: organisations need to give guidance which is clear, practical and relevant. They need to be explicit on what can and cannot be worn and they need to think about how much of the corporate brand is communicated through employees. There needs to be alignment. Organisations aren't valued for their buildings, land or inanimate objects; organisations are valued for their people. So many companies leave employees to work out what is 'appropriate dress code'. Left to their own devices it's easier to get it wrong than to consistently get it right. They need to wake up to this fact and invest the time and effort to provide appropriate advice.

I have a client which is a highly successful organisation in the technology/telecoms industry. They have an extraordinary brand in a mature market. I often work at their offices and I am continually struck by how appallingly dressed many of their staff are. They look as though they're going to the beach, the garden or a club. They certainly don't look as though they're ready to do business. And the brand values that are being projected through their image aren't good ones – or ones which compliment their corporate brand, come to that.

Business Casual Image Wreckers

Let me start with some 'dos' and 'don'ts' for business casual, which have nothing to do with the choice of clothes – that comes later.

DO NOT:

(i)   Slacken on your personal grooming. A five o'clock shadow at 9am, greasy hair, a worn-out manicure and wearing no make-up all look dreadful and project a brand of their own. Ladies: an aside if I may on the subject of no make-up. At 21 we could fall out of bed, brush our hair and look okay. Beyond that age, very few women can. Get over it. I'm not talking about layering it on with a trowel. I am talking about a tiny bit of blusher, mascara and lip gloss as the absolute minimum.

(ii)   Think, 'It'll do'. It usually doesn't. If you don't make some effort when you're dressing on a 'business casual' day not only will it show, but it will project a brand which is lacking consistency, attention to detail and care.

(iii)   Wear what you would to do the garden or the supermarket shop. It will look exactly as if that's where you're headed.

(iv)   Try for a nanosecond try to excuse your choice of attire by virtue of the fact that your colleagues don't bother so why should you? This one particularly confounds me. You're not 12 and in the playground now. You're a successful professional who realises the importance of commercial brands. You want to stand out from the crowd for the right reasons, not blend in with everyone for all the wrong ones.

(v)   Believe that dress code guidelines are an attempt by a corporate machine to clone everyone. They aren't, and it isn't an excuse to look dreadful in business casual, or any other code of dress come to that.

(vi)   Choose any item of clothing on your lower half which allows the rest of the world to see what underwear you're wearing. Low cut trousers are chief offenders in this category but it's not a look that's appropriate in a business setting – ever. The same effect (or worse) can be achieved if you're not careful with linen (even dark coloured garments can become transparent in certain light and reveal underwear colour if it's not a flesh colour.)

(vii)   Wear excessive jewellery (I don't particularly mean the 'medallion man' look here but I do mean too much 'jangling'.)

(viii) Wear flip flops and, for gentlemen, open-toed footwear.

(ix)   Combine bare legs with short skirts. If you add to this the fact that they are bottle-white, un-groomed and on the large side, that would be particularly unappealing. An aside for ladies: I often have resistance from my female audience when raising the spectre of bare legs as part of the list of image wreckers. The point I'm making is this - you have to be careful to align not hijack your brand through your image and this can easily be done with bare legs. If they are slim, toned, a fabulous colour and beautifully groomed you have to be careful about having too much of them on show. What will the rest of the world focus on? What you're saying and your professional capabilities or your fabulous legs? I will admire beautiful legs as much as the next man, but too much of them on show and it's simply just not the right look for doing business.

(x)   Wear white socks.

(xi)   Wear cheap-looking shoes.

(xii)   Go to work with bare shoulders (too sexy is the brand message here). And, the other issue is that it can reveal the underarm grooming equivalent of road-kill.

(xiii) Show too much cleavage. What does 'too much' actually mean? Again, what are we primarily focused on? If the eye goes (and tends to stay) at your cleavage then it's too much. Also, beware of the danger of clothing that falls forward if you lean over at all – thereby revealing an eyeful.

(xiv)   Allow bra straps to be visible.

(xv)   Reveal hairy legs (especially when housed in flesh coloured tights so that we can see the length of the hair up against the leg in all its glory). Yuk. Don't think it doesn't happen. It does. I worked with a very successful executive at a FTSE company who had this particular issue.

(xvi) Wear trainers. These project a brand which is about casual relaxed and young. Don't wear them to work – unless there's a gym at the office.

(xvii) Wear clothing which needs attention. This covers a multitude of sins but ranges from missing buttons, split seams, partly down hems, creased, stained or dirty clothing or shiny items in need of the dry cleaner.

(xviii) Wear clothing which is too tight – so what one's eye is immediately drawn to is the horizontal folds (which means too tight). Tight skirts, trousers, shirts, trousers, blouses and jackets look awful.

(xix) Wear trousers which are too short. This is by far one of the most common image wreckers that I see, amongst both men and women. Trousers should fall to mid-heel of the shoes most often worn with them. Unless, obviously, they're designed to be Capri trousers or three-quarter length, for example. Ankles should never be visible. The correct length of trouser is one that falls on the shoe with a slight fold.

(xx) Wear clothing which is too big – this creates vertical folds and causes equal damage to your look.

(xxi) Neglect shoe maintenance. Shoes are an expression of our economic status. There are so many expressions in our language which reflect the importance of footwear within our psyche. 'Down at heel' has its origins in the human behaviour which says that we check out the back of someone (all the way down to their feet) as they leave the room. The quality and condition of our shoes reflects so many brand values – not least of which is attention to detail. Gentlemen's shoes should always be highly polished and shiny (if leather) or smartly brushed (if suede). Tips and heels should be regularly maintained. Ladies – a similar message for you but an additional consideration is the state of your heel tip. The sight of a worn-through heel tip with the back of the heel leather curling up ruins your appearance. The metal tapping sound of your shoes should also give an audible clue to the need to get them repaired. The other general image wrecker around shoes to be mindful of is the 'driver's heel'. The left heel will wear and appear scuffed if the same shoes are used to drive.

(xxii)   Wear wayward ties. A tie should be tied so that the tip just touches the waistband and the knot (whichever your preference) is neat, balance and at the top of the shirt, overlaying the top button. Any deviations can project an appearance of slapdash, too casual and poor attention to detail.

(xxiii) Wear garish ties. Gentlemen, express your personality by all means through your choice of tie. However, beware of ruining your look rather than make a statement; it screams offence.

(xxiv) Wear button-down shirts with a suit and tie. I've never liked this look, chaps. It screams 'no style' and 'no idea'.

(xxv) Wear colours that don't suit your natural colouring too close to your face. There is a myriad of shades of white shirts – some will suit you and others won't. If you've never had your colours analysed then this is an investment which, truly, will last a lifetime. If you're wearing the wrong coloured clothing or accessories (or make-up for ladies) then you will look pale, tired, older and worn-out. That will be the brand message you communicate. Not an appealing thought, is it?

(xxvi) Show off tattoos. I have to mention these not least because of the growing trend for body art, particularly in the UK. Tattoos typically elicit a strong reaction in us (good or bad). The point is: in a business environment, unless your business *is* a tattoo parlour I would strongly argue that putting these on show can wreck your image. I have a client who employs a lady who has the first line of her football team's anthem (in Latin) across her lower back. Each to their own of course, but she insists on wearing low cut trousers, with tight, higher cut tops that ensure it's nearly always on display to the rest of the world. What is that all about? It screams 'look at me', or more specifically, 'look at my tattoo'. What is the brand being projected here? In non-work time what you put on show is entirely your choice – but in work time, keep them covered.

(xxvii) Display body piercing - another area of controversy and a potential image wrecker. Pierced ears for women do not usually cause any difficulties; neither do nose studs (providing the stud is suitably small). The problems tend to start (gentlemen, I'm sorry about this), when men wear earrings for work. There is a brand associated with earrings for men and it's not a good one. What comes to mind for you? Interestingly, men tend to have a stronger negative reaction to other men wearing earrings in a business environment. Ladies, the image wrecker for you around body piercing is navel rings which are on show. A flat stomach with a pierced belly button does look great, but not in a work environment. The brand communicated says sexy, which in other contexts is great, but not when you're at work. Cover it up ladies. A momentary aside since we're talking about the belly, if I may. There has been a shifting fashion trend towards having your tummy exposed through lower cut trousers and tighter fitting tops. Even if you have a flat, toned stomach, it's not a good look in business, but if you're carrying weight in this area then it *really, really, really* isn't a good idea – in any context. The whole 'jelly belly' look is ghastly. Always.

DO:

In many ways, the 'dos' are the converse of the 'don'ts'. However, in addition:

(i)   Invest in some quality items to create a capsule 'business casual' wardrobe. My tailor calls it investment dressing and I think he's right. By quality items I primarily mean quality of the fabric (and fit). Gentlemen – if you are going to wear shirts, I'd still advise the same quality shirts that you might wear with a suit. But obviously it could have a different colour (e.g. button down) or more colour or print to it.

(ii)   Aim to look sharp in business casual rather than just 'okay'. Is looking 'okay' good enough? That's a case of being dammed with faint praise if ever I heard it. And by the way, if you answered 'yes' to my question then raise your expectations of yourself a notch or two. You're worth it.

(iii)   Pay the same attention to your grooming as you would when attending an interview. Your brand is still as important on an everyday basis as it is when you're overtly going after a new job opportunity.

(iv)   Take extra care with your choice of clothing and accessories during warm weather. Like it or not, we are experiencing hotter summers and milder winters, and that can wreak havoc with your personal brand.

Tidy Casual

What a great name for a code of dress! (As opposed to 'untidy casual' or 'anal retentive casual'). What I will describe here is not appropriate business dress. The clothes I mean here are jeans certainly worn with other clean, pressed separates. Boots of any sort, trainers, flip flops all would work here, as would linen or at the opposite end, chunky knitwear. Belts, bags and jewellery can be a large, small, coloured, chunky, patterned and causal as you like. Rucksacks, knapsacks, bum bags all abound here. This is making an effort – but definitely a casual look. It could be the occasion where you're going to a lunch party, for a picnic, to the pub, to watch a sports match. I know what you're thinking now. 'Yes, but what if I'm doing one of these events with my clients or colleagues?' Corporate sponsorship of football, cricket, rugby and other major sports means that you could well find yourself in a freezing cold stadium on a windy Saturday in November. Clearly you need to be comfortable, but also you need to be credible (in business terms). So make more of an effort and be certain that all your clothing and accessories say 'quality'. The same rules about right fit and right colour also apply. Remember, like it or not, you can't hide from the fact that your brand is affected if your client sees you dressed like a football thug or bouncer on Saturday afternoon and then is talking business with you on Monday morning. Ultimately the reason you're at the match for business first and foremost. Consistency is king. Ignore that at your peril.

Casual

And finally, the code of dress defined as casual. This means no effort. Zilch. Nada. You can roll out of bed and on to the sofa to watch television in your pyjamas; holey, stained, painting T-shirt; your underwear or baggy running bottoms for all I care. The clothes don't have to be clean, pressed, your colour, made in the last ten years or indeed follow any of the rules I've talked about already. These are garments you'd wear to garden, work out, relax at home, carry out DIY, sunbathe or go to the supermarket. And no - never, ever, ever, ever, think you'd be able to wear these clothes for work. Ever. Forget it.

The Only Thing That Separates Us From The Animals...

.....is our ability to accessorise. One of my 'Power of Six' factors behind looking good is the notion of current. I mention that at this point because accessories can make or break your look. Accessories are an excellent opportunity to reflect your personality and your brand. Do you want to be known as creative, though-provoking or edgy? Or perhaps classic? Refined? Sophisticated? They are your brand values – so keep them firmly in your mind when choosing shoes, briefcases, man bags and wallets.

(ii) Complementary

If you look in the mirror and think 'I look fat, too barrel-chested, too short, too tall, huge in the rear end, etc.' then join the rest of us. The fact is simply this: if you don't like what you see in the mirror then the clothes you're wearing are wrong, not the body. Looking good in what you wear is more a matter of balance and proportion than height and weight. As an image coach, my goals are to help my clients create optical illusions through their clothing. Certainly, if you want to lose weight, tone up, become more in shape, get rid of your beer belly and so on before going shopping for new clothes then that's absolutely fine. But don't let your current physical imperfections stop you from looking good (and feeling good) *now*. The word to keep in mind when considering 'complementary' is the f-word: 'fit'. If it doesn't fit you properly then it won't look complementary to your actual (rather than imagined) body shape.

And by the way, the importance of fit holds true whether or not you have a phobia of exercise *or* if you look like someone who's just run off the set of *Baywatch*. Refer to the ladies' and gents' size 'dos' and 'don'ts' guide overleaf for more information.

Ladies And Gents Size 'Dos' And 'Don'ts' Guide

	DO	DON'T
PETITE (5' 2' OR UNDER)	Go for vertical emphasis. For example, stripes or single blocks of colour. Direct attention to the face or upper body half with eye-catching jewellery, ties or neckwear. Single-breasted suits will work better (if the correct scale) because they add the illusion of height.	Break up the line of sight with contrasting coloured belts or shoes. Wear clothes that are too bulky or too heavy. Wear accessories or patterns that are too large because this will accentuate your lack of height. Wear turn-ups on trousers.
TALL	Focus on horizontal emphasis, such as necklines, tie patterns, belts and horizontal designs on your clothes. The line of sight will	Wear vertical stripes or dress in a single colour as this will only accentuate your height. Wear small prints and small scale accessories or

TALL (continued)	DO	DON'T
	travel horizontally and distract from your height. Contrasting shoes and hosiery works well for ladies. Use turn-ups on trousers as these will shorten the leg on suits (gentlemen).	patterns on clothing, shoes and bags, all of which will also draw attention to your height.
LEAN	Go for horizontal emphasis on clothing and accessories. Double breasted jackets, wide lapels or necklines and detail on the buttons will work well. Palazzo or wide-cut trousers or bias-cut skirts/dresses	Wear too tight clothing as this will accentuate your leanness. Wear pencil skirts (ladies) and tight fitting trousers (ladies and gents) and anything that is too long (jackets, coats, sleeves and skirts). Single breasted jackets will only accentuate your

LEAN (continued)	DO	DON'T
	will all work. Clothes which add bulk (e.g. cargo trousers, heavy/bulky sweater fabric) can be worn.	slimness.
LARGER FIGURED	Go for dressing mono-chromatically (i.e. in a single colour). Gentlemen, pin stripe suits will look better on you with a single breasted jacket. Ties should have vertical or diagonal stripes. Ladies, vertical emphasis on necklines, jewellery and scarves works well.	Gentlemen, horizontal stripes will add emphasis in the wrong way. Wear double breasted suits. Ensure your clothing fits properly. There's nothing worse than ill-fitting clothing to accentuate size. A half-size too small will mean looking a whole size bigger.

Why The 'F Word' Is So Important

I want to return to the importance of 'fit' again. When you shop for clothing what part does the sizing label play in the whole purchasing decision? Are you one of those women who never buy an item of clothing bigger than a size 10, for example? Just because come hell or high water you're not going to get bigger by allowing bigger sizes into your wardrobe? Or are you a gentleman who is resolutely a size 36" waist, despite the fact that you've not actually measured it in the last decade? Here's the reality of what goes on – not just in the UK, but also in the American shopping mall and in clothing retailers all over the world. If you took the same size garment from three different stores and tried them on, they would all fit you differently. Why? Because retailers cut their garments differently.

Italian-designed clothes for women, for example, tend to be cut very small and you have to buy bigger sizes relative to the equivalent in the UK. You haven't suddenly become a lot heavier overnight – it's just a reflection of the garment's cut. Fact number two: if you always tend to shop in the same store (or couple of stores) every year, then the same size garment will change its cut. Again, why? Because retailers are very sensitive to the (literally) changing shape of the population and are keen to accommodate that fact. The UK is currently suffering an expansion – literally – in its average waist size. Quite simply the size written on the garment may bear little relation to your body shape. Hence, you have got to try it on.

Petite women are already wise to the single best investment you can make when buying clothes – a good tailor. In the UK, if you are a 'typical' size 14, you cannot expect every size 14 garment to fit your particular shape. There are literally millions of other women who would say they are the same size – but they're not all going to be the same shape – so alterations (particularly for your investment pieces) will be necessary. The same principle holds absolutely true for gentlemen.

Pause For Thought

- What have you learned from the material you've read so far?

- What are the key insights to note?

- Are there any actions you should take as a result of this learning? You can note them on the personal brand action plan at the back of this book or put them somewhere you will definitely be prompted to actually do them.

(iii) Colour

Essentially colour theory, whilst not an exact science, reveals that for both men and women the following is absolutely true: we look healthy, refreshed and fabulous wearing some colours close to our face but tired, drawn and old when wearing others. There are a number of different systems which have been developed to help us understand colour, its characteristics and impact on our lives. This book is not about critiquing the advantages and disadvantages of each system. However, I will talk a little about the system which I use to work with my clients and in which I was initially trained.

Interestingly, colour analysis has suffered as a 'brand' itself because it became synonymous with trying to get everyone into canary yellow or peacock blue. The expression 'having your colours done', (which by the way sounds as bad as what you put your pet through if you don't want them to reproduce), was associated with being lightweight, irrelevant and vain.

You can't *not* respond to colour. Colour affects our mood, appetite and blood pressure and is absolutely all-pervading in our lives. Essentially colour has three different qualities or characteristics when understanding the simple question 'which colours suit me?'

The first is the characteristic (or direction) of *depth*. This is simply the notion of how rich or concentrated a colour is. A second quality or characteristic of colour is *undertone*. All colours have either a blue or yellow base (unless it's a true colour). A person who suits colour with a blue base or cool undertone will have the potential for an ashen look (especially when ill). A person who suits colour with a yellow or warm undertone will project a golden glow (e.g. freckles, even with pale skin). Finally, (and by the way I've listed these different characteristics in no particular order of importance – that is revealed within the colour analysis, because it always depends on the individual), is the notion of *clarity*. Quite simply this is to do with how bright, sharp or vivid a colour is versus whether it is more dusky, muted or subtle. A person who will suit bright colours will have a bright, sparkling look and their eyes often support the 'bright' appearance. A person who will suit muted colours will have little or no contrast between their eyes, skin and hair.

Don't try and work out your direction from this (very) brief summary of the different directions. It doesn't work like that. A colour analysis with a trained image professional will enable you not only to appreciate which characteristics or qualities of colour are most suited to your natural colouring, but also the priority of importance. It's the price of a decent meal out, but the investment will last for years and not play havoc with your waistline either. Don't confuse the description of colour characteristics with brand. Wearing deep colours no more communicates a deep thinker than wearing blue communicates you're a hip, happening, cool kind of guy. It's the impact of wearing the right (or wrong) colours that affects your image and your personal brand. And that's what is important to know; and if you don't – find out.

My following comments on colour 'dos' and 'don'ts' relate to colour that we wear close to our face. Remember that you can wear whatever colour you like on the lower half of your body.

Colour 'Dos' And 'Don'ts'

DO	DON'T
Find out what is your 'best' white. And then invest in work shirts, blouses and quality T-shirts in that colour for your business and casual wardrobe.	Dismiss the importance of having at least a rudimentary understanding of your own colouring and which colours to keep close and away from your face.
Ensure you have a suit, coat and at least one sports jacket from your palette of best neutral colours.	Know what I mean by 'palate of your best neutral colours?' You should do. Get your colours analysed.
Take your colour swatch or an item which you wish to co-ordinate with a new purchase, when going shopping for clothes, accessories or cosmetics.	Buy an item to colour co-ordinate with existing garments based on your memory. We don't remember colour accurately in our mind's eye and you'll waste time, effort and probably money.
Go for high-colour contrast for occasions when you want to communicate personal brand values of authority,	Wear brown to any interview. Think that's weird? We don't connect brown with authority, presence or credibility in

professionalism or credibility through your image.	these situations. So ditch the brown suit that day please.
Go for low-colour contrast for those occasions when you want to communicate personal brand values of approachability with clients and colleagues.	Have either a couple of colours only or kaleidoscope of colour in your wardrobe. It could well be that you're wasting money and wardrobe space. Stick to the qualities of colour that suit your best and build 'capsule wardrobes' around these colours.

Colour and Brand

Every colour has its own brand values associated with it. I've listed below some of the brand values associated with each colour. This comes from research undertaken in Western society and shouldn't be assumed to translate across the entire globe.

RED	Powerful, dynamic, assertive, successful, aggressive, demanding
BLUE	Intelligent, professional, trustworthy, conservative, credible, aloof, cold
GREEN	Harmonious, approachable, empathetic, trustworthy, boring, bland
PURPLE	Creative, innovative, confident, good

	quality, authentic, successful
ORANGE	Youthful, dynamic, fun, energetic, abundant, immature, frivolous
PINK	Youthful, empathetic, approachable, innovative, feminine
WHITE	When combined with a deep shade: authoritative, assertive, powerful. When worn on its own: empathic, approachable, pure
BLACK	Authoritative, assertive, powerful, sophisticated, oppressive, menacing
GREY	Reliable, respectable, efficient, lacking energy and confidence
BROWN	Serious, respectable, supportive, empathetic, approachable, creative

So now what? Well, information is power is all I'm saying. Some of the adjectives used to describe these colours are found in your personal brand values. Don't get so 'hung up' on colour that you literally can't see a way forward, but at least armed with this information you can make more informed choices. This is particularly true when there are occasions at work where you are looking to influence in a certain way. Colour theory can certainly help support; rather detract from your efforts.

(iv) Wardrobe Personality

I don't mean by this whether or not you're kind, thoughtful, interesting, selfish, dull or boring. I'm talking about what image experts term your 'wardrobe personality'. In other words, how you reflect the role which clothes play in your life through your choice of attire? Do you dress for comfort? Or to make a statement? Perhaps it is to co-ordinate classically. Or to express your creative side? Or perhaps your wardrobe personality simply represents the fact that you don't really care that much about clothes as they aren't that important to you. Take a look at the descriptions and see which describes you most accurately. We all typically have one or two dominant personalities, although may have outfits which could reflect more than this in our wardrobe.

Classic: You like a co-ordinated look with a classic, timeless quality to your clothing. You like to be co-ordinated and appreciate clothing and accessories which represent quality. Your challenge may be for the 'business casual' or 'casual' part of your wardrobe as you might find it hard to 'dress down'.

Expressive: You like expressing your personality through your clothing and appreciate the colour, shape and feel of clothes and accessories. You may have artistic or creative tendencies! Your challenge may be dressing for those occasions which require a formal, professional look.

Natural: You may have little interest in fashion and see clothes as a necessity for comfort rather than for style. You prefer a sporty or very casual look rather than what you perceive as starchy, formal business wear and so wearing suits or very professional attire may be a challenge for you.

Dramatic: You like to make a statement through your clothing and like to be noticed. You appreciate bold tailoring, colour, design or detail on clothing and accessories. Whether for business or casual, you like to make a statement and your challenge will be to ensure that the statement isn't too distracting for your audience.

Gamine: You have a small frame and hence require appropriately sized clothes to fit you properly. You appreciate wearing colour and may consider neutrals quite dull. Your accessories and fabric pattern and detail should be in proportion with your size and this represents your biggest sartorial challenge.

Coming back to the notion of personal brand, what does this all mean? In simple terms, wardrobe personality is important because it says that we don't all look the same or should try to look the same, even when given the same dress code guidelines. Equally, it must be said that image experts aren't trying to get you to dress in a uniform fashion either, (a common objection that I hear when working in the corporate market). If you maximise your brand through your clothes, then you will want your clothes to make the right statement about you and your personality. What you want to ensure you avoid is a contradiction or disconnection between the brand values you want to project, and your preferences around wardrobe personality. Flexibility will be key.

(v) Well Groomed

The Personal Grooming Audit is not intended to offend. The reality is that we can all probably think of someone or some occasions where we ourselves either noticed a personal grooming malfunction, (which sounds like a Janet Jackson Super Bowl explanation by the way), or had one ourselves. It happens. The issue is: do we care enough to want to minimise the chances of experiencing these in the future? I assume we do – hence why you're reading this book and this section. So have a go at the audit, have a giggle, be honest and more importantly, reflect on what you've learned by completing it. Is there any action you can take? If so, what is it?

Personal Grooming Audit: Gentlemen

QUESTION	YES/NO
1. Do you wear a clean, pressed shirt (formal or casual) for every day at work?	
2. Do you use mouthwash, whitening toothpaste and dental floss regularly?	
3. Do you wash your hair every day?	
4. Do you dry clean your suits regularly?	
5. Do you have a different pair of shoes to drive to work from those you wear on arrival?	
6. Do you have (and use) a personal grooming kit at the office (e.g. toothbrush, toothpaste, deodorant, and comb).	
7. Do you hang your clothes out to air before returning them to the wardrobe?	
8. Do you always check your appearance in a full-length mirror before leaving home?	
9. Do you have dandruff?	
10. Are your nails neatly clipped?	
11. Are your nails dirty at this moment?	
12. Do you suffer from razor burn?	
13. Do you visit your dentist regularly?	
14. Do you clean your shoes at least every other time they are worn (especially in winter?)	
15. Do you wear any clothing to work that has seen better days? (e.g. holes or extensive bobbling in jumpers; shirts with frayed cuffs or collars; jackets or trousers which require some repair; or any item of clothing that just needs to be washed?)	

Personal Grooming Audit: Ladies

QUESTION	YES/NO
1. Do you regularly polish, re-heel, re-sole and re-tip your shoes?	
2. Do you use mouthwash, whitening toothpaste and dental floss regularly?	
3. Do you wash your hair every day?	
4. Do you dry clean your suits regularly?	
5. Do you have a different pair of shoes to drive to work in from those you wear on arrival?	
6. Do you have (and use) a personal grooming kit at the office (e.g. toothbrush, toothpaste, deodorant, brush, cosmetics).	
7. Do you hang your clothes out to air before returning them to the wardrobe?	
8. Do you always check your appearance in a full-length mirror before leaving home?	
9. Do you have dandruff?	
10. Are your nails neatly manicured?	
11. Are your nails dirty at this moment?	
12. Do you clean your shoes or boots at least every other time they are worn (especially in winter?)	
13. Do you check the state of your make-up (and re-apply as necessary) during the day?	
14. Do you visit the dentist regularly?	
15. Do you visit the hairdresser regularly?	

Scoring For Personal Grooming Audit

Question Number	Gentlemen : Points per Question	Ladies : Points Per Question
1.	Yes = 2 No = 0	Yes = 2 No = 0
2.	Yes = 2 No = 0	Yes = 2 No = 0
3.	Yes = 2 No = 0	Yes = 2 No = 0
4.	Yes = 2 No = 0	Yes = 2 No = 0
5.	Yes = 2 No = 0	Yes = 2 No = 0
6.	Yes = 2 No = 0	Yes = 2 No = 0
7.	Yes = 2 No = 0	Yes = 2 No = 0
8.	Yes = 2 No = 0	Yes = 2 No = 0
9.	Yes = 0 No = 2	Yes = 0 No = 2
10.	Yes = 2 No = 0	Yes = 2 No = 0
11.	Yes = 0 No = 2	Yes = 0 No = 2
12.	Yes = 0 No = 2	Yes = 2 No = 0
13.	Yes = 2 No = 0	Yes = 2 No = 0
14.	Yes = 2 No = 0	Yes = 2 No = 0
15.	Yes = 0 No = 2	Yes = 2 No = 0

0 – 16 : You have some work to do to ensure your grooming doesn't let you down. Don't think it doesn't matter – it does and it's noticed. A lack of grooming can do untold damage to your personal brand so it's time for you to make some changes.

18 – 24 : Some good work on your personal grooming but there are one or two lapses which occasionally let you down. Identify the areas to work on and make the changes. A small amount of effort will really pay dividends.

26 – 30 : Congratulations! Your personal grooming is excellent and your challenge is to maintain it. So, a place to start might be taking a look at the one or two rare occasions when you have a lapse.

Being well groomed is about personal grooming as well as the grooming of your clothes and accessories. Think about it for a minute. How much time and effort would you put into your grooming when attending an interview? Or going to a wedding? I love talking with professionals about this concept because it usually initially causes some ruffling of feathers. However very quickly my clients appreciate the fact that their grooming may not always be of a consistently high standard. Remember, having a brand around 'well groomed' relates to brand values of reliability, attention to detail and commanding respect before you open your mouth. Can you still look well-groomed when you're running late, have a pressing deadline or have been up for three hours in the night with a sick child? Consistency is key here. We all have days with personal or sartorial grooming challenges (broken zips or buttons, travelling on the tube in the summer etc. etc.)

Allan Pease wrote a book called *'Definitive Guide to Body Language'* and in it he talks about the triangle of influence represented in the upper part of your body. Imagine an inverted triangle, which covers your face and shoulders with the tip finishing about mid-sternum. Pease's studies revealed that this area, along with your hands, represents a significant triangle of influence when we communicate with others – especially for the first time. We take in their eyes, hair, skin, teeth and hands and the information received is processed to create impressions by us of others.

Skin Care

This isn't the domain solely of women. The male grooming market, and skin care products specifically, have been identified as an area of significant economic growth. Men in the UK are now spending twelve times more on grooming products than they used to. (As an aside, I am convinced that a fair chunk of this is the responsibility of a dear friend of mine's husband – who has an extraordinary predilection for shampoos, shower gels and the like. There was a time when he had literally dozens of lotions and potions in his bathroom.) It seems that gentlemen have woken up to the fact that it's not just women who shed their skin every thirty days. If you are someone who does nothing to look after your skin and it still consistently looks clear, bright and smooth then you are one of the fortunate few. For the rest of us, if some care isn't taken to look after it then it shows. And it's not a good look.

Gentlemen have to additionally contend with the trials of shaving, and if you are a chap who suffers from razor burn then don't just put up with it. There are plenty of products on the market to soothe your skin and remove this distraction from your face. In terms of your personal brand it's not about being vain or self-absorbed, it is about being consistent, especially if you want to project personal brand values of quality, care, attention to detail and attractiveness for example.

Teeth

Most Americans believe that Europeans have dreadful teeth and, by and large, they've got a point. In the UK we can't put this down to our chain-smoking history because we are now a largely nation of non-smokers.

Yellow teeth and bad breath mean poor dental hygiene and this is a revolting turn-off. I used to work with a chap who had the most raging halitosis. I simply couldn't bear to be near him and rarely paid any attention to anything he said because I was trying not to pass out amidst wave after wave of offensive odour when he spoke. What struck me most profoundly, when I finally shared the facts of my halitosis with him, was the genuine shock and utter surprise with which he received the news. He had absolutely no idea. (If you've received some feedback akin to this, or indeed any other area of personal grooming then believe me, someone has done you a massive favour. Don't ignore it. Act on it.)

Good teeth are definitely worth investing time and effort in, and I do mean time and effort as opposed to cosmetic dental work, unless you've left it too late and have no other choice. So go to a good dentist twice a year and use a high-quality whitening toothpaste, an electric toothbrush (especially if you're partial to red wines, curry, ketchup or smoke), and always floss and use mouthwash.

Heavenly Hands

I'm talking about the state of your hands, rather than what you do with them. One of the questions from my Personal Grooming Audit was simply, 'Are your nails dirty at this moment?' Have you got dirt lodged under the nails? Are your nails neat and clipped (or manicured)? Or are they rough and uneven? Your hands and their condition reflect how much attention to detail you pay, (and whether your nails are clean or not is a mirror of how well and how often your wash your hands). If you like DIY or gardening for example, don't let your hands be an advertisement which reflects this fact. Your hands need to look as though they're ready for business – along with the rest of you, so take appropriate steps to protect and look after them.

Shaving versus Facial Hair

You might think it odd to talk about this topic. However it's surprising how often I see appearances wrecked by poor care in this area. If you are a gentleman who gets a five o'clock shadow by 11am, you may want to consider keeping a shaving kit at work. After all, what are the brand values associated with a 'not shaven today' look? Someone who overslept? Worked all night? Someone who can't be bothered and/or doesn't care how they look?

If you sport a moustache and/or beard, keeping these in good condition is also important. The grizzly bear look only really works on... a grizzly bear. I find food and drink appear to provide endless possibilities for sartorial chaos with beards and moustaches. Keeping food remnants for later is vile to look at and most of us are too polite too say anything. Remember, if you want to be known for quality, attention to detail and exceptional customer care for example, you can't square this with food or drink captured in your beard or moustache.

And on the subject of hair a note to gentlemen (and ladies occasionally) – beware the curse of nose hair. If we don't check and keep it in trim (literally) there can be plenty of personal embarrassment. Especially if you (i) have a cold or (ii) have been out in the cold and then come inside. Enough said. You get my point. Let's move on.

Hair Care

I think – if travelling by public transport in the UK recently is anything to go by – there is a tidal wave of dandruff sweeping the nation. If you suffer from this condition, and there can be a host of different causes for it, then invest in a decent medicated shampoo, check collars throughout the day (it's particularly obvious against dark colours), and do not ever go a day without washing your hair. If the problem isn't controlled through these strategies, seek help from the medical, homeopathic or alternative medicine profession. Rampaging dandruff wrecks your image and completely contradicts brand values of care, attention to detail and quality.

Hair Loss

Although largely the domain of men, I do have one female client in her forties who suffers from this condition. I certainly don't wish to diminish the effect of this for chaps, it is more widely socially accepted that this fate befalls a large proportion of the male species. (For women this condition is extremely tough, as hair is supposed to be a woman's 'crowning glory'). The issue in relation to brand is how you deal with it. Do you embrace it? Enhance it? Deny it? Hide it? The latter two strategies are very hard to successfully implement and much time, effort, frustration and money can be wasted in the process.

Think of some well-known public figures who have attempted, but failed, to do the same thing. Why have they failed? If you've noticed their (failed) attempts to deny or hide their hair loss, that's not a good start. In terms of brand, what's the impact? It's too easy for your hair loss to become part of the definition of who you are, and this to be the ultimate irony given your best endeavours to distract others from your hair loss. Harsh as it sounds; your hair loss will always be a much bigger deal for you than it is for anyone else. Talk to your barber or hairdresser about a cut which makes sense for the shape of your face and changing hairline.

Hair Colour

I went grey at 22. A number of my clients don't have a grey hair on their head well into their fifth decade. Moving past my deep personal loathing for them, the area of hair colour is an interesting one for both men and women. What brand values spring to mind when you think of a man with grey hair in a business environment? Experienced? Distinguished? Wise? Possibly. What brand values spring to mind when you think of a woman with grey hair in a business environment? Is it the same as for men? Well, unfortunately not, it would seem. Grey hair (unless a particularly glorious shade which isn't that common), is associated with being old, out of date, frumpy and out of touch. This perception is compounded if you haven't had a decent cut recently, don't wear make-up and don't take time to invest in clothing that suits your body shape and colouring.

When 'Warming You Up' Washes You Out

If you're going to invest the time and money in adding colour to your hair then a word of warning. I hear time and again highly skilled, highly trained hair professionals encouraging their clients to go for colour that will add 'warmth' to their hair. This sounds a great idea doesn't it? However, as the section on colour suggested, this will not look good if you're a lady or gentleman with cool colouring. Hair professionals are not usually trained in the theory of colour in the same way that image professionals are. This is not in any way a side swipe at the industry – far from it. My point is simply this: if you are going to go for hair colour – invest in a colour analysis first. The knowledge and information gleaned from that session will last you a lifetime and will ensure that you don't waste resources on a hair colour (which then needs refreshing regularly), that does nothing to help you achieve the effect that you are looking for.

Roots

If you go down the route (sorry no pun intended) of colouring your hair it represents a commitment to regular hair maintenance. Visible roots are a classic image wrecker – especially when there is a strong contrast between the bottled hue and you natural hair colour. Dark roots showing through on blond hair look particularly bad. It looks cheap, tired and in dire need of some work. I know I keep saying your brand needs to be consistent – but there's a reason why. That means you hair should always look good, rather than be absolutely fine one week and suddenly not good the next. Dependent upon the speed at which your hair grows, make sure that your hair colour (and condition which can be badly damaged with long-term colour and chemical styling) always looks good.

Care of Your Clothing and Accessories

One of the things I'm paid to do is spend time in my clients' wardrobes. Undoubtedly there's a joke about coming out of closets but let's move on. Looking after your clothes isn't a case of being anally retentive with no significant interests in your life. It makes financial common sense. Decent clothes cost a decent chunk of change and they can last a lifetime and ultimately represent incredible value for money –

if you look after your clothes properly and wear them regularly. It's ridiculous to spend large sums of money on expensive suits or jackets, but then hang them up on cheap, wire hangers that will damage your clothes and cause them not to look their best on you when next they are worn.

Wardrobe Wisdom

DO	DO NOT
Hang your suits or separates out of the wardrobe overnight on the day after wearing them, in order that they may air properly.	Store clothes in the plastic covers after collecting them from the dry cleaners.
Use wooden or moulded plastic hangers for jackets, shirts and tops.	Use wire hangers – ever.
Use hangers with clips to hang trousers upside down and in the line of the crease.	Put clothes away dirty. Dirt attracts moths and other unpleasant inhabitants to your wardrobe.
Keep moth repellents in the wardrobes.	Fold trousers over a hanger.
Use wooden trees inside your shoes and boots, especially those worn often for work – they will last longer and look better.	Put clothes back in the wardrobe if they require dry cleaning, ironing or mending. Get that done first.
Hang the same types of clothing together. For example, jackets next to each other, shirts next to each other, trousers next to each other and so on. It encourages you to mix and match more effectively rather than always wearing the same two separates	Hang sweaters or cardigans on hangers. They should be folded and kept in air-tight storage.

together.	
Store accessories (shoes, belts, bags) so that you can see what you have.	Forget that your feet sweat in your shoes. Use a deodoriser before returning them to your wardrobe.

The Bottom Line on Personal Grooming

It's hard to overdo personal grooming and easy to slip up on it. Remember more than anything, your brand perception can be seriously damaged by poor grooming. It's what you become defined as – 'Mike with raging halitosis' or 'Sharon with permanent lipstick on her teeth'. Brands are about consistency and this is no more true than in the area of personal grooming. If you do, it helps project quality, credibility, reliability and is very, very attractive!

(vi) Current

This does *not* mean being trendy, scouring fashion magazines every week, having the latest 'it' bag, or wearing ghetto street clothing. It means staying in touch with current fashion leanings *without* being a slave to it. In relation to personal branding this is actually very significant. If your look is out of date, what does this say about your thinking? The analogy which I often use relates to the film *'Wall Street'* with Michael Douglas. If you're old enough to remember it, (and perhaps even recall seeing it at the time), then I would suggest that when Michael Douglas (or his alter ego Gordon Gekko), picked up and used his mobile 'phone during one scene, *at the time,* you will have thought nothing of it. However, if you were to take a look at that film now, you would undoubtedly notice the telephone. It's the size of a brick with an antenna last seen on the international space station. It looks outlandishly dated and absurd now. That's the point about ensuring our image remains current. Try out my simple self-audit quiz and see for yourself.

Ladies – you particularly need to beware of looking out of date. It's a great example of where our personal brand, as projected through our image, is brought into sharp focus. And it's not fair that men can get away with it more easily than we can. If we look old, tired, out of date, what does that say about our thinking? Back to one of my 'power of six' factors – the need to be current.

Are You Current Or A Cliché?

How current is your approach to your appearance? Answer questions in the relevant column and find out!

GENTLEMEN	Yes/No
1. Is it more than four years since you updated the frames for your spectacles?	
2. Have you got a hairstyle that hasn't changed in more than five years?	
3. Do you have significant sideburns?	
4. Do you wear a lot of jewellery?	

5. Have you sported facial hair (moustache/beard) for more than five years?	
6. Do you own suits that are more than five years old?	
7. Is your mobile phone more than three years old?	
8. Does your briefcase look a bit battered?	
9. Do you wear the same pair of shoes with every business outfit?	
10. Do you tend to buy your clothing and shoes from the same shops all the time?	
11. Do you own jackets with leather patches at the elbows?	
12. Do you always wear white shirts and rarely/never any other colour shirt?	

LADIES	Yes/No
1. Is it more than four years since you updated the frames for your spectacles?	
2. Is it more than three years since your changed either your hairstyle or hair colour?	
3. Do you wear navy tights?	

4. Do you tend to wear the same pieces of jewellery all the time?	
5. Do you tend to stick to the same lipstick or eye shadow most of the time?	
6. Do you own a brass-buttoned blazer?	
7. Do you tend to co-ordinate shoes with bags?	
8. Do you wear shoes with a cone-shaped heel?	
9. Do you wear scarves with everything?	
10. Do you tend to buy your clothing and shoes from the same shops, year after year?	
11. Do you use one handbag for most, if not all, occasions?	
12. Do you tend to stick to wearing the same colour clothes?	

So what? The point is simply this – if you have answered 'yes' for more than two questions from the audit, then you need to beware that you don't look out of date from time to time. Keep those brand values in mind and as always, make sure there isn't a conflict.

The Last Word (Nearly) On Image And Personal Brand

You may be surprised to see just how many pages of this book are devoted to image. That's for a good reason. There's a lot to discuss. Really. If you've not already done so, now it's time to start identifying your actions from the ground covered so far. Supporting your brand positively through your image means focusing on the 'Power of Six'. So here are six summary messages for each:-

(i) Appropriate: Different levels of dress code communicate different brand messages. Remember the golden rule: It's easy to turn a more formal look into a more casual one – with the same clothes. However, it's impossible to turn a more casual look into a more formal look with the same clothes.

(ii) Complementary: The importance of *fit* can't be over emphasised! A capsule wardrobe of ten items that fit properly will create a far greater impact than lots of ill-fitting clothes.

(iii) Colour: Think about how colours can support your goals in terms of image. Contrast dark and light for maximum authority, remember the role of brown (gentlemen) in a formal business setting and consider how your own colouring works well with some colours more than others.

(iv) Reflect Your Personality: You can and should reflect your personality through your image. It's not about being a 'clone' with your business look, but always remember who's trying to do the influencing.

(v) Well Groomed: Don't have a 'day off' when it comes to personal grooming. Always be consistent and immaculate.

(vi) Current: You don't have to be trendy but you *do* have to be current. Why? Because otherwise you will have some brand conflict. Accessories can give you away here.

Pause For Thought

- What have you learned from the material you've read so far?

- What are the key insights to note?

- Are there any actions you should take as a result of this learning? You can note them on the personal brand action plan at the back of this book or put them somewhere you will definitely be prompted to actually do them.

Chapter Three
Walking the Talk

Shake That Booty : Body Language

We can recognise over 250,000 different body language signals without even realising it! Do you remember studying all these at school? Of course not. However, we've learned them all the same. You'll be relieved, as am I, that I don't intend to cover all of them and explain their impact in relation to your personal brand. No one's got that kind of time. However what I will do is talk about a few of the most common ones and offer some general comments in relation to how they relate to your personal brand. The reality is that people rarely think consciously about the effect of many of the seemingly simple non-verbal things they do.

There has been some interesting research which revealed that our average total talk time in a day is between 10 and 15 minutes. Note that I used the word 'average'. Clearly there will be days when we talk for longer – and days when we talk less. It doesn't seem very much does it? Particularly given the fact that we're awake for typically more than 14 hours a day. What was meant by this statistic was simply that if you added up every single word spoken in a day (and timed how long it would take to say them all), between 10 and 15 minutes is the total amount of time it would actually represent.

The Rules of the Game: The 3 Cs

We are typically not great at reading body signals because we become distracted by the words spoken. The schoolboy errors committed when interpreting body language are due to not following the rules of the game – otherwise known as the '3 Cs'.

Rule Number 1: Clusters

The first rule is clusters. In other words, the mistake is to take one gesture in isolation and interpret it – irrespective of other gestures or circumstances. So for example if I fold my arms, it could mean any number of things. I might be cold, I might be uncomfortable, I might not agree with you, etc. The point is simply that interpretation of a single gesture is nonsensical. The metaphor used by anthropologists is that it is like taking a word without the rest of the sentence. Take the word 'form'. A cursory check in the Oxford English Dictionary revealed 13 different definitions for it. You get the point about clusters in any case.

Rule Number 2: Congruence

There has been some research to suggest that non-verbal signals carry about five times as much impact as verbal communication and when the two are incongruent, many (especially women) rely on the non-verbal message above verbal content. So, look for congruence between what they are *saying* and what they are *doing*. Often I'm asked 'can you fake body language as part of building rapport?' Typically 'NO' is the answer – unless you're intentionally really, really, really good at it (which we aren't).

Rule Number 3: Context

All body language should be read in the context of which it occurs. Do you remember the award winning advert for the Guardian newspaper which ran in the 1990s? It featured a skinhead (i.e. young man with shaven head, tight jeans, bomber jacket and Doc Martens), who ran towards a smartly dressed businessman walking down the street. You assume as the viewer that the businessman is going to be mugged, but in actual fact the skinhead is saving him from walking under some falling bricks. The advertisement was shot in slow motion and in black and white to heighten the effect of the unfolding drama. The strap-line was, 'It all depends on your point of view'. Therefore, make sure you're taking in the whole view! You need to see the whole context so that your view isn't distorted or misinformed.

Handshake High Noon

A professional gesture which you will repeat thousands of times in your career is the activity of shaking hands. It has always struck me as bizarre that we rarely (if ever) receive feedback on our handshake, and yet it is such an important component of our brand. One of the activities which I run when delivering corporate training is to 'mix up' my handshake when greeting delegates for the first time. For some of the audience it will be suitably firm, of the right duration and my palm will be cool. Then, I will affect a limp-wristed, sweaty palm when shaking hands with other members of the group. When the course reaches the point where we cover handshakes in relation to personal brand, I will ask the group who remembers mine and what it was like. After initial reticence, it's always the ghastly handshake that is readily recalled. And what were some of the brand values that it communicated? 'Weak', 'ineffectual', 'underwhelming', 'unprofessional' and 'surprising – not in a good way' were some of the impressions created by this ineffective gesture.

It's back to my shop window analogy again when it comes to personal brand. If your handshake is a good one (and I'll define that in a moment), then you've at least ensured that the other person doesn't have cause to form initially negative first impressions of you and your capability. So, they, to return to the analogy, either want to continue to look at the shop window or maybe go in and browse. However, if your handshake is poor, then you've succeeded in installing some negative impressions which may take a while (or not – they may remain long term), to change. The shopper has decided to carry on walking past your shop window, or goes into the shop under duress, having decided that the merchandise is going to be poor quality.

This may sound like an odd request, but I'd encourage you to go and seek some specific feedback on your handshake. In order for this to be a useful thing to do, let me be specific about what you are looking for from those with whom you shake hands.

(i)   Hand Position: Fairly self explanatory – where and how is your hand clasped in relation to theirs?

(ii) Grip: How firm or loose is your grip of their hand?

(iii) Duration: How long does the handshake last and what is that like for the other person?

(iv) Temperature: By this I mean heat and moisture.

Get comments from several different sources and ideally make sure you shake hands with both sexes.

Handshake Heaven and Handshake Hell

The whole point of a handshake is that it signals the start of a warm, positive and friendly exchange between you and the person whose hand you are shaking. Part of your brand has to be 'approachable', or, at the very least, 'able to do business with'. It's the basis of building rapport. So, two key ingredients are needed here – firstly that both hands are in the vertical position so that no one's hand is either dominant or submissive. Secondly, apply the same pressure as you receive. If you were meeting a number of people at once, you should expect to have to alter the intensity and angle of the handshake to create a feeling of rapport for each individual.

Remember: men, you can on average exert twice the pressure of women (you shake harder) – so be mindful and make allowances!

The golden rule: unless you and the other person have a personal or emotional bond, only use a single hand. Who should reach out first? You should consider a couple of things before initiating the handshake. Am I welcome? Is this person happy to meet me or am I forcing them into it? What are the cultural considerations? (For example in Muslim countries it would be completely inappropriate).

Handshake Heaven	Handshake Hell
Offer your palm in a vertical position to be shook – always.	Offer your hand with the palm facing downwards. It is extraordinarily aggressive and likely to cause offence. Why? The gesture implies dominance on your part, and the recipient is going to have to work very hard to establish equality within the interaction.
Be flexible with the grip and duration of your handshake.	Assume a vice-like grip. Indeed there is a handshake with this very name. Inflicting

	discomfort (or even pain) at the point of physical contact seems at best unfortunate and at worst insanity. Your brand will be significantly damaged and you'll have to work hard to repair it. Warm and friendly is needed at this point.
Always smile and introduce yourself by your full name (if it's the very first meeting) as you shake hands.	Become a mute when shaking hands.
Stand up or remain standing to shake hands. You are more likely to literally (as well as metaphorically) set the relationship off on the right foot.	Remain seated if the other person is standing when shaking hands. Again, this creates an instant inequality in body position. It will only be okay if both parties remain seated.
Be willing and confident to initiate a handshake. Think what this says about your personal brand. There's even some research to suggest that women who initiate a handshake will create a	Wait for the other party to initiate a handshake. Get stuck in.

more positive first impression.	
Take steps to remedy your palm if you know it is warm or clammy. Tissues or wet wipes are very effective – particularly if you know you're prone to this (we all are).	Effect a clammy, sticky handshake. The brand association is weakness and lack of effectiveness.
Be confident to 're-do' a handshake if it misses the mark. For example sometimes the fingers are grabbed rather than the palms. Be gracious and smile but suggest that you try that again.	Fall in to the trap of using other dominant behaviours around the handshake because you believe it will create the right impression. It usually doesn't. Examples include excessively pumping the arm (2-3 times is usually sufficient), grinding the knuckles together, trying to yank the person towards you or remaining steadfast in your spot with a stiff arm.
Move towards the other person once you have decided to shake their	Use two hands. Its brand association is dominance and unless a familiar situation, I'd steer well

hand.	clear. It's highly likely to offend.
Clasp the palm firmly but not too tightly and beware of rings!	
Beware of cultural differences with handshakes for different parts of the world.	

When The Other Person Clearly Doesn't Know What They're Doing...

It's been a while since I've voyaged out on an aside so I will do so now. It's well overdue so please bear with me. I notice quite often when working with professionals how heated they can become when engaged on the topic of people whose hellish handshake they've experienced, particularly – gentlemen forgive me – in relation to handshakes between men where a dominant palm is offered. There are a number of different suggestions offered as to how to deal with this. They include a complicated 'step to the right' technique, putting your palm on top of their downward facing palm, refusing to shake hands or simply adding their handshake to the list of reasons to hate them forever more in all future professional interactions.

All of these strategies have the potential for embarrassment, confusion and discomfort. If you want to be perceived as assertive without being aggressive, confident without being dominant or friendly without being patronising, then my suggestion for demonstrating grace under pressure in this 'dominant handshake' situation is simply this: accept the downward facing palm but quickly use your other hand to help guide the palm to a vertical position and remove the second hand instantly. If it lingers, it will become a two-handed shake you will have made the point, and if you combine this with a genuine smile and eye contact then you are least likely to offend. The other party will experience your point – as would you if your palm had been turned through ninety degrees. I think this is an opportunity to be graceful under pressure. Remember, most of us have never had feedback on our handshake and are blissfully unaware of whether it is good, bad or indifferent.

To Kiss or Not To Kiss?

That is the question. This is a whole (relatively) new area of business etiquette that has come to the fore and it is significant in relation to your personal brand. Across the business world all kinds of chaotic, confusing and on occasion embarrassing scenes are played out in relation to kissing colleagues at work.

My sense is that there are a couple of different scenarios in relation to kissing where a distinction needs to be drawn before I go any further. My thoughts are based on Western European culture and I appreciated and will comment on the international perspective a little later on. This also means that I'm not going to talk about men kissing men (which would be relevant in certain parts of the world.) For you I'll assume at this point that a decent handshake is all you need to know how to do.

Meeting A New Colleague, Client Or Contact For The First Time

Don't kiss them, try to kiss them; think about kissing them or wonder what it would be like to kiss them. It's not appropriate. You've just met. You don't know them. Although clearly you want to focus on building rapport and creating a basis for a warm and friendly relationship, to kiss them isn't the way to do it. Focus instead on making sure your handshake is right. I've said more than enough about handshakes a few pages back if you've not yet taken a look. I have seen, and experienced, many a bewildering moment when a complete stranger has leaned in to kiss on first meeting. It's too forward, presumptuous and invasive of the other person's personal space and professional preferences. These are not brand messages that you want to invoke. Ever.

Meeting Colleagues, Contacts Or Clients Once Again

This whole area is a minefield and I appreciate how tricky it can get. I have several organisations as clients who have a strong 'kissing' culture. I have forged strong, professional relationships with a number of my contacts and, whilst it wouldn't be my personal preference, they like to express hello and goodbye via a quick peck on each cheek. I have decided to take that as a compliment; I honestly don't mind and actually, I think it would damage the relationship now if I said I did. I can live with it, and I guess that's my point. It has to be a personal choice on your part. If you don't want to kiss the other person, then don't – even if it is a 'kissing culture'.

Naturally I have (as I'm sure you do) clients who would rather spit in your eye than kiss or be kissed and to even begin to initiate this specific behaviour within their culture would cause problems. I did say all this kissing lark was a minefield. However, if you are going to kiss, a couple of dos and don'ts, if I may, only because I keep seeing this happen and these suggestions apply whether it's kissing going on between the sexes or between ladies.

DO	DON'T
Go for cheek-to-cheek rather than lips-to-cheek. Excess saliva or a lipstick mark on your colleague isn't a good look and it doesn't feel that great either.	Kiss under duress. It shows.
Ensure you don't reek of garlic, curry, overpowering perfume or aftershave. You're about to invade their personal space	Ever, ever, ever, ever kiss lips to lips. That privilege should be saved for your significant other, your

in a big way and they'll notice the odour and remember it.	children and perhaps your granny.
If you're going to double kiss go for left to right (as you look at the other person). It's how we read and is the typical way our eyes travel horizontally in Western culture.	Ignore the other person's body language. If they're 'saying' non-verbally that they don't want to be kissed – then leave it well alone. Smile instead!

Kissing With Confidence

Is it one kiss or two? Or even three? Which cheek do you start with? Do you actually kiss them or is it more a cheek-to-cheek kind of movement? I told you it was a minefield. The fact is that you need to pay attention. In the UK, people who have a predilection for kissing colleagues at work tend (not always) to go for one kiss. In mainland Europe it's two kisses (one on each cheek) or sometimes even three. In the Middle East it can be three or more (and men kiss each other too). In the USA, if someone wants to go for more than a handshake, then it tends to be a hug, rather than a kiss. In the Far East, there is not the emphasis on kissing at all instead there are other nuances to the greeting with potential to build rapport or cause huge offence.

Not Kissing With Confidence

What if you really don't want to be kissed, but have a horrible feeling that a colleague is looking to plant a smackeroonie on you imminently? There are simple steps you can take to make the message clear (without being so obvious as to say, 'Oi! Leave it out mate or I'll knock your block off.')

(i)   Smile and take a step backwards

(ii) Move your body so that you use more 'closed' rather than 'open' body language

(iii) Maintain a rigid lower arm when shaking hands

(iv) Take the lead and offer a hand to shake rather than loiter, hoping not to be kissed

The bottom line: unless they are people that you know socially or would consider a friend, then don't do it. If in doubt, don't do it. They won't be offended if you *don't* kiss them; they may well be offended if you *do* and they didn't want or expect it).

Here's Looking At You Kid

Oh come on! Of course I was going to name a section about eye contact after one of the most famous lines in cinematic history. Our language is peppered with expressions about this behaviour, (seeing eye-to-eye on an issue, eyed him up and down etc.) which only serves to reinforce the importance of eye contact in relation to building your personal brand. If you think about it, making direct eye contact with another person is one of the most intimate connections you can make with your clothes on! Our eyes are, as the saying goes, the windows on our soul. So what's your eye contact like? What do you notice about other peoples? And what impression or brand does that start to build for you about them? Is someone who looks at you constantly deemed in your eyes (see what I mean!) to be 'aggressive'? 'Domineering?' 'Intense?' Or what about someone who avoids eye contact with you? Are they thought to be 'shifty'? 'Rude'? 'Immature?'

There are several different ways in which we look at other people which I discovered when researching this book. You might want to identify which types of eye contact you most often engage in.

The Social Gaze

Experiments into gazing reveal that during social encounters the gazer's eyes look in a triangular area on the other person's face between the eyes and the mouth for about 90% of the time. This is the area of the face we look at in a non-threatening environment. The other person will perceive you as non-aggressive. This is the ideal approach for maximising your personal brand in business.

The Intimate Gaze

This is a function of being a human being. We all do it so don't deny it. Apparently what happens is that when we approach another person we quickly move our gaze between the other person' face and lower body and then back to the face. This is called the ogling gaze – what an apt name! Women have wider-ranging peripheral vision and so can get away with it more easily than men. Men's tunnel vision (which means head moves up and down) means they get caught. The point of mentioning it was that I thought it was fascinating research, but also relevant to personal branding. Perhaps you can think of someone who does this a little too often. And what do we associate with it? Nothing which we would want when it comes to defining our personal brand values in a professional context.

The Power Gaze

Imagine the person has a third eye in the centre of their forehead and look in a triangular area between the person's three eyes. The impact of this has to be experience to be believed. Not only does it change the atmosphere to very serious, it can stop a bore dead in their tracks. Provided your gaze doesn't drop below the eyes the pressure stays on them.

The Power Stare

If you have soft, wimpy or weak eyes practise using the power stare. This means trying not to blink when maintaining eye contact. Narrow your eyelids and focus closely on the person. If you move your eyes from person to person it has an unnerving effect on those watching you.

The Extended Blinker

A normal, relaxed blinking rate is six to eight blinks per minute and the eyes are closed for only about a tenth of a second. People under pressure, for instance when they are lying, are likely to dramatically increase their blinking rate. Extended blinking is an unconscious attempt by the person's brain to block you from their sight because they've become bored, disinterested or uncomfortable or they feel superior! With their eyes shut for two to three seconds or longer they wipe you from sight and remain closed as the person momentarily removes you from his/her mind.

I had one client who demonstrated this behaviour. His reasons were shyness and habit. The impact it had was damaging and distracting.

Eye to Eye

Interestingly some data, and training that I've researched for this book, suggests the maxim of maintaining strong initial eye contact on first meeting someone. However, this can causes problems. *Why?* Because this is contrary to the process that we would typically go through when meeting someone for the first time. Typically, a man wants to check out a woman's hair, legs, body shape and overall presentation. If she maintains eye contact then he's faced with having to steal glances during the meeting (and getting caught). Women do the same thing but because of their peripheral vision, rarely get caught.

The Solution?

Allow a two or three second window after shaking hands in order for this process to be completed. From there on in, for most cultures, to build a good rapport with another person, your gaze should meet theirs between sixty and seventy percent of the time. When we talk we maintain forty to sixty percent eye contact and an average of 80% when listening, except Japan, some Asian and South American cultures where it's considered disrespectful or even aggressive.

Smile And The World Smiles With You...

It would not make any sense to talk about eye contact and *not* mention our smile because these two components of our face are critical in influencing others and certainly an important part of your brand. Do you smile at work? What about in business situations? Do you think smiling is a sign of weakness or appeasement and therefore deliberately don't smile often? Do you hate your teeth? (A reason regularly given by my clients and again harks back to my suggestion of investing in some decent dental work.) Our smile can be engaging and an aid to rapport or it can be off-putting, even disconcerting if it's not a genuine, natural smile. Generally smiles are recognised as an expression (however fleeting) of happiness and it's hard when faced with someone smiling at us not to reciprocate. That's because smiling behaviour is linked to a mirror neuron in our brain – we mirror what we see. (It's like yawning. Have you ever noticed that when you watch someone else yawn you have an irresistible urge to yawn yourself? You may even be yawning as you read this. Anyway, I'm sorry. I digress. Back to smiling.)

So what's your smile like? Is it an asset to your image and brand? Or is it something you've never really thought about? A genuine smile, with decent teeth, is always appealing. A false smile or a flash of ghastly teeth is repulsive. So, take a look at your smile in the mirror or in photographs. What's it really like? If you really don't like your teeth then for goodness sake, get the work done. It is always worth the investment because they're life-long. You'll get your money back that's for sure. It strikes me as bizarre how often people are quite prepared to ignore their teeth (and they may be crooked, riddled with fillings or yellow), but are quite happy to spend far more money on anything from a car to a pair of curtains.

Strut Your Funky Stuff

You learned to walk at around two years of age, give or take. Outside of some possible parental reminders when you were a truculent teenager, your walk has had no further attention or feedback since. So, it's been a while. If you want to see what I'm getting at, just pay attention to how people walk for the next day or so. Sit and watch the world go by for a few minutes and then you'll see what I'm getting at. How you walk says a lot about how you are at that moment in time. It also says a lot about your personal brand. If you shuffle along with your head down, shoulders hunched over and laden down with stuff you tend to carry around with you, then that hardly says confident, purposeful, dynamic and able to see the bigger picture does it? You should walk with your back straight, your head up, and your eyes forward with purpose, confidence and contentment, even if you don't fee it. The act of walking in this way will change your state so you will feel (even if it's marginally) better.

Heads Up

Have you ever thought about how the use and position of your head is a very persuasive tool in your personal brand toolkit? There has been some research to suggest what we're communicating via the position of our head. For example, the reason why a lot of adverts have women with their head at an angle (thereby exposing their necks) is because it's seen as a submissive gesture, and they appear less threatening or confrontational. If you want to be known for being a great listener, this is a gesture that's widely recognised as being associated with listening – so it might well be something you want to use.

If your head is down then that's universally associated with appearing dejected, disapproving or disinterested – so there's no good news with that one. And we reflect our interpretation of our head position in our language – which is why 'chin up' means encouragement to feel more positive. Interestingly, if you are in a role which requires regular commercial negotiation then you will undoubtedly be aware of the importance of keeping your head up so that you're communicating parity with the other party.

Resting Position

One activity I will encourage my delegates to explore in my image workshops relates to their most comfortable postures or 'resting positions' when they're at work. Of course we move through a range of different body positions during the day dependent on our level of engagement, hunger, interest, fatigue and temperature; however you might want to consider what the most comfortable 'resting position' is for your body. When you're relaxed and engaged how do you tend to position yourself? What are you communicating through your 'resting position'? That sounds like a good piece of feedback to seek from those whom you trust, by the way.

Imagine, ladies, being dressed to the nines in a fabulously cut suit but sitting in a slouched, cowered position with your head down. Are you communicating personal presence, confidence and inner strength? Hardly. Gentlemen, you need to beware of appearing too aggressive, and the posture that reflects this most profoundly is your hands clasped behind your head with one leg bent at 90 degrees resting on the opposite knee is the worst. It appears to be open and welcoming, but actually it is interpreted as a false attempt to encourage you to relax your guard, before being metaphorically attacked. It's also a very male gesture.

Ladies, for you the challenge is to avoid appearing too much like a little girl. By that I mean legs wrapped endlessly around each other, or a hunched physique, crossed arms and head down. All of these are a no go. It says 'don't hate me'; 'don't hurt me'; 'protect me'. Well, unless that is what you want to communicate (I think not), then experiment with ways to be comfortable but also congruent with your personal brand values.

Chapter Four
Behaviour That's Bad News

Personal Brands And Business Behaviour

There are numerous excellent books out there on the topic of business etiquette. I'm not going to write a mini-version of another one here. What I will do is suggest seven of the most disrespectful, off-putting or even downright infuriating habits in business. If you recognise any of these, then make breaking the habit part of your action plan. It's doing untold damage to your personal brand. I have tested these theories on a wide range of professionals in business, and believe me, they resonate.

The Seven Bad Habits Of Highly Ineffective Personal Brands

Habit Number One : Married to a Mobile

Are you one of these people who are permanently attached to a mobile gadget (be it a telephone, Blackberry or a Bluetooth hands-free device) and insist on email, texting and taking calls during meetings and/or conversations? Do you realise how rude that is to the other people you are with? That's why voicemail was invented. You can't do both activities well at the same time. They've got professional lives too and if you can't pay them the courtesy of your full attention for the duration of the call, then you should know that they have better things to do with their time than watch you talk/text/email someone else in their company. And if you think it's okay to do this because you're not required for all of the meeting, then why are you there?

Your time isn't being used efficiently and you could be much more productive by shortening the call or removing the meeting from your calendar. It's a bad business habit and my maxim is this: would you expect your biggest lead or most important customer to tolerate this behaviour? What about the managing director/CEO? Would you behave in the same way in front of them? If they shouldn't have to put up with it, neither should anyone else.

Habit Number Two : Lazy and Late

Are you someone who tends to be late for conference calls or meetings? Certainly we all have the misfortune to be late *occasionally* when the world conspires to prevent us from getting to where we need to be – but that's why I used the word 'occasionally'. It doesn't happen very often. One of my clients is the managing director of a very successful international organisation who was extremely focused on her team, and her employees, being on time. Her maxim was this: 'I pay people to work – not wait'. She had a point. I've also known professionals in my career who are incredibly relaxed about being on time (as in: they never were and didn't care what impact it had on people waiting for them). Two words that don't come to mind in relation to their personal brands are 'courteous' and 'respectful'. And it doesn't scream 'team player' either. The 'lazy' part is because they've never fixed this habit (which is what it is) and may or may not have really considered the impact it's having on others. This kind of behaviour is highly damaging to a personal brand. Get a watch, get organised and get to calls and meetings on time.

Habit Number Three : Lousy Listener

Are you a good listener? If you immediately answer 'yes' then think again. There is a wealth of evidence out there in business publications to suggest that listening is one of the lowest capabilities which professionals have. We hear – on average – 25-30% of what is said. Why? A number of different reasons including the assumption behind this perceived-to-be-passive skill that because we have two ears, we're listening. Mostly we're not. We just look like we are, or – if we're not good at that – we're clearly showing that we're not listening. Not convinced? Try my self-assessment and judge for yourself. Tick those statements that are true for you. Be honest!

Listening Self Assessment

Statement	✓ or ✗?
(i) I prefer talking to listening.	
(ii) I sometimes assume what the other person is saying and will finish their sentence for them.	
(iii) As soon as I know what I want to say during a conversation, I am then focused on adding my bit to the discussion as quickly as possible.	
(iv) I sometimes think that certain people aren't worth listening to.	
(v) There have been times when someone was talking but I had no idea what they said because I was distracted.	
(vi) I often interrupt the other person whilst they are talking.	
(vii) I may appear to be listening to someone, but sometimes I am thinking about something or someone entirely different.	
(viii) I sometimes completely misunderstand what was said and have to explain the reasons why I said what I did.	
(ix) I may formulate a conclusion while someone is talking and will interrupt to	

suggest it.	
(x) I keep talking after interrupting someone and may continue until after they have stopped.	

If you've ticked even one box, that means you've got some work to do on your listening skills – especially if 'good communicator' or 'exceptional customer service' (for example, but there are others) are part of your personal brand.

Habit Number Four : Problem Producer

Are you a problem seeker or a solution finder? I used to work for a boss who always said to me that she had no difficulty with her team coming to her with problems, as long as we brought our suggested solutions too. Do you know what doing a 'YP' is? YP stands for 'your problem'. It's a slightly more civilised way of saying that you are dumping your problems on someone else to fix and waiting for them to come back to you when they have done so. If you manage others, it's not a great example which to lead and encourage in others. In terms of your own brand, make sure you're not a 'YP' kind of person. It reeks of someone who lacks creativity, situational leadership and personal responsibility.

Habit Number Five : Swear You Don't Swear

Do you use bad language at work? Yes? No? Sometimes? What are unacceptable and acceptable swear words for you? (An aside: I worked with a client recently who had some feedback as a result of a 360° assessment conducted for the leader within his business which suggested that two of his team deeply resented his expression 'for the love of God'. He would use it when expressing frustration specifically. His direct reports were offended by the use of the term 'God' because of their profound religious beliefs. It's not easy is it?)

Anyway, back to the point. I fully appreciate that if we care about what we do that means we're emotionally involved in it. There are days when we feel let down, fed up, angry, irritated, de-motivated, disinterested, sad, tired, etc. In terms of branding, the rules are simple: don't swear – ever. It's crude, rude and absolutely not clever. And that's the worst part. If you want to express your frustration – then do so by being clever but polite – it has far more impact. The reason for using Oscar Wilde as my opening quote to this book was his ability through the characters in his plays, to be scrupulously polite – even when actually being insulting. To scream, shout or use language otherwise heard on a football terrace in any work context does not fit with a brand which wants to be known as 'professional', 'inspiring' or 'graceful under pressure' (amongst others).

Habit Number Six : Bore For Britain?

Whatever happened to the basic art of good conversation? Are you able to strike up an easy, natural discussion with someone you've just met? Or do you get tense, clam up and appear acutely uncomfortable? As successful professionals, but also as successful people, being able to conduct a decent conversation is vital to the success of your personal brand. Quite simply, you've got to be able to talk easily with others without it becoming tortuous, tedious or tetchy. I'm regularly surprised at the lack of conversation skills I come across.

These include folks who:

(i)   Ramble on incessantly about their achievements, their job, their children, their opinions and their life in the deluded view that it's fascinating and engaging to the listener. Quite frankly *no one* is that interesting.

(ii) Become mute, unable to mumble anything above a syllable.

(iii) Become lazy and simply expect you to do all the work during the conversation

(iv) Take this as an opportunity to impart their knowledge on every subject under the sun to you at every turn. I particularly dislike know-alls.

Good conversation is like watching a game of tennis – there's got to be some to and fro. I talk to for a bit, then you talk for a bit, I ask questions, you answer and vice versa; I listen, you listen. It's a *shared* activity in every sense of the word. Poor conversation skills are off-putting at best and highly damaging to your personal brand at worst. Learn some basic conversation etiquette (use open questions, don't interrupt, share information about yourself – but not too much too quickly, smile, etc.), use good eye contact and non-verbal nods for encouragement.

Habit Number Seven : Forget you're at work when you're at play?

You're always communicating your brand at work – even when you're not working. One of the biggest causes of brand damage occurs when we socialise with our colleagues and clients – be it at conferences, dinners, team nights out or corporate entertainment. The potential for catastrophe is huge. I've seen many a cool, calm, collected professional turn into a cold, aggressive and/or tearful alter ego after too much drink. A female colleague of mine was charming, attractive and articulate at work but became incoherent, loud and revolting when drunk. It is simply horrible to watch and the death knell to her credibility in a professional environment. Don't ever be one of those people who wakes up the next morning and thinks 'what did I do?' That says it all – you lost control and that's very poor in a work setting. It's never funny (for you) even if you did moon at half the company on the bus back to the hotel. People have long memories.

I ran a workshop with a marketing team of young, bright and successful individuals – all of whom had been out with one of their agencies the previous evening. They had a great time (fair enough), but there was one lady who was late and all she could say throughout the day was 'I'm hung over'. How good does that sound? It doesn't. We're not in the student union bar now and there are no prizes for the depth or longevity of your hangover. She was continually redefining her personal brand and blissfully ignorant of the damage she was doing to it. Don't make the same mistake.

Remember my rule about standing out from the crowd for the right reasons, not blending in (with the other drunken, immature idiots) for the wrong ones. You're always at work when you're with colleagues or clients so you should always represent the brand values you want others to perceive about you. *Otherwise, how you behave socially becomes how you're defined professionally.*

Dating At Work

The other area to mention, which isn't a bad habit but which is more difficult simply because it's more common, is how to handle meeting someone else who may become a significant other (and if it's a fling then my following comments are especially relevant). If we don't meet our partners at school, university, through an interest or at a social event then the chances are we'll meet them at work. The point is simply this: your love life is no one else's business, however if you conduct a 'work' relationship in front of everyone else, your personal brand will not do well out of it. Why? Because your brand becomes redefined by who you're having a relationship with.

It might not be right, or fair, but that's how it is. Is that what you want? People can and do judge, and it's often not kind (including men talking about other men). Even if the organisation has a relaxed view about personal relationships at work, keep all of that away from public view (a particularly good strategy if the relationship doesn't subsequently work out). I'm not saying don't have relationships at work, I am saying keep it to yourselves.

Pause For Thought

- What have you learned from the material you've read so far?

- What are the key insights to note?

- Are there any actions you should take as a result of this learning? You can note them on the personal brand action plan at the back of this book or put them somewhere you will definitely be prompted to actually do them.

Chapter Five
Language and Personal Branding

Talk, Talk, Talk

The final part of your shop window on which to dwell is what comes out of your mouth. You can look great, behave non-verbally in a very influential way and then let the side down entirely with what you say. There comes a point where what you say has a dramatic impact on the perception of you and your professional capabilities. It has to. So, I will linger here only briefly (because I did say at the beginning this was a book you could read in a couple of hours), and consider some of the most significant components of your verbal communication which impact your personal brand.

Let me begin by positioning a couple of caveats. The one (hopefully not wild) assumption I will make is that the content of what you say is okay. This might not be the case of course (and if you receive this feedback it would be a foolish and arrogant person who simply dismisses it), but even so, I'm not going to talk about *what* you say – instead I am going to talk about *how* you say it.

Secondly, I fully realise that when you wish to build rapport with another person it makes sense to flex your language to match (in an authentic way) how the other person is speaking. I don't mean suddenly trying to copy their accent or 'rubbish' words, but you may certainly want to consider flexing speed, tone, language and use of the pause for example.

During my image workshops I may record an individual's speech and play it back to them. (By the way, have you ever had this experience on prior training programmes or wedding videos and the like?) Isn't it true to say that you sound very different to how you *think* you sound? This is precisely why I encourage you to go and seek feedback from those with whom you communicate most often – but not without being clear on what it is about which you want their comments. Specifically:

(i)   Speed
(ii)   Tone
(iii) Pauses
(iv)   Jargon
(v)   Rubbish Words
(vi)   Accent

Speed

Do you tend talk at a hundred miles an hour? Or are you more like the tortoise than the hare when it comes to speed of speech? Obviously I've pulled out a couple of extremes here – but we all have a predilection and it would be useful to understand that

– particularly given that when we're under pressure because those situations are when we will tend towards our preference. If one of your brand values is 'poise' for example, that doesn't sound right if you talk at a hundred miles an hour. Equally, if you want to be known for 'dynamism' that doesn't work well if your speech is slow or laborious.

Our speed of speech may in part be affected by others' response to it (back to what I was talking about earlier regarding head nodding for example). Or, it may be affected by the content or context (e.g. providing a detailed, complex technical briefing to the team or, presenting to an auditorium of 500 people would be two such scenarios).

How does our speed of speech alter when we're under pressure? We need to be mindful of this, and if necessary, learn to speed up or slow down. Why? Because one of the occasions when we might feel under pressure is an occasion when we want to communicate our brand in a very positive way – such as interviews, pitches and presentations.

Tone

How would you describe how you speak? Verbal tone is impacted by accent most certainly. We attach a lot of values around verbal tone because it's something we notice very quickly. Whatever your accent, and I'll talk more about that later, do you sound interested and engaged? Variation in our verbal tone is associated with these descriptions whereas monotone is associated with boring, bored or dull.

Beware of brand conflict. As always, the content and occasion may have an impact here; but get some feedback – *if nothing else on your voicemail message.* In fact, call your own phone and listen to yourself. How do you sound? Is it aligned with the brand values you want to communicate? This is a powerful tool for giving a great impression to whoever hears it and, my goodness, there are some extraordinarily bad ones out there.

Pause

You may think this an odd thing to include in the components of *how* we speak, but it's important. Why? Think about it. If you can hold the attention of the audience whilst saying nothing that shows how effectively you've engaged them. It's an extraordinarily powerful tool to have in your communication toolkit and if your personal brand is 'powerful communicator' – then you should be very good at this. You don't want to pause just for the sake of it – that's absurd – but you do want to be able to command the attention of your audience, whether it's in a conference call, at a face-to-face meeting or at a keynote presentation, so that they are keenly waiting to hear what you want to say next.

Jargon

This covers a couple of things. Consider certain sections of the professional services world for a moment. Management consultants have suffered historically with a very definite brand association (whether it's right or wrong is not the point) in this area. The notion of using phrases like 'put this on the back burner'; 'run it up the flagpole and see how it hangs'; 'pushing the envelope'; or my personal favourite: 'mission critical issues in upstream operations', are all examples of metaphorical language which has the potential to confuse, distract, irritate or amuse. It's jargon, euphemism and nonsense when used in the wrong context with the wrong individuals. Do not be persuaded that it implies increased intelligence because it doesn't. Unless you are working with people who use this sort of language all the time and you wish to influence them more effectively (which is absolutely fair enough as a strategy), then beware the damage it can do to your personal brand.

Some organisations and industries (perhaps you work for one?) suffer from acronym overload. 'The MBB for TIP is on an AST for Q1' is an expression that I remember well. Mainly because I had absolutely no idea what on earth this particular client was talking about and I subsequently lost the will to live. All organisations develop their own lexicon, which is a reflection of their culture and this is entirely understandable and acceptable. Naturally you need to be comfortable and confident with this lingo when influencing colleagues. However, beware, beware, beware when abbreviations become the mainstay of sentence construction. It may be meat and drink to your colleagues, but it's the death knell to communicating effectively with clients, prospects, suppliers and anyone else who doesn't work in the same business as you.

Rubbish Words

These are simply words or phrases that add absolutely no value whatsoever to what you're saying. Any word said too often is actually a rubbish word because we have eroded its original meaning through over use. Outside of excessive (we all say these from time to time) 'ums' and 'errs', I would add expressions including 'sort of like', 'do you know what I mean?' and 'at the end of the day' to the list. I once worked with a lady who just peppered her language with the phrase 'sort of'. In one five minute period I counted 'sort of' a total of 105 times. And that's the point. A rubbish word is not only a verbal irrelevance, it's also incredibly distracting. As a result, the listener may switch off and just start counting the rubbish words, (for the fun of it or to release the tension of hearing a phrase endlessly repeated which they would rather not). A male client actually came to see me because one of his personal brand challenges was that he had become known within his organisation as 'cut and paste'. That's what he was renowned for saying by his peers and colleagues, and he had to rid it from his language. So don't think your personal brand won't suffer. It will.

Accent

The subject of accents tends to evoke a strong response amongst my clients. I didn't plan to mention it; however I'm regularly asked about it. Personally I love the richness and diversity of them. If you want your personal brand to reflect the fact that you come from a certain part of the country then that's great. Having a great personal brand is *not* about trying to sound like a BBC Radio 4 continuity announcer – authenticity is critical for everyone and if that's not you, then don't try and make your accent something it isn't. My comments in relation to accent have in part already been mentioned – the issues around verbal tone and speed for example.

The point about accents is when they have a capacity to cause confusion *or* if what you say creates a negative brand perception. Let me be specific. If your accent uses a word or expression that isn't used by other parts of the country, then it can distract the listener or cause them to switch off from the rest of what you're saying because they don't understand what you've said.

My other note of caution relation to accents is this: pronunciation. If there is one element to accents that does cause the hair on my neck to stand up it's when words aren't pronounced correctly. I don't mean the age old north/south divide in the UK around vowel pronunciation (e.g. 'bath' and 'barth' for the device you bathe in). What I *do* mean is when accents are known for pronouncing words in a way that simply isn't correct. For example a 'th' is pronounced as an 'f'. There's no 'f' in 'thanks', 'Thursday', 'think' or 'through'. Another example might be missing the 'g' on the end of words, such as 'happening', 'going' etc.

Or adding a 'g' to a word which doesn't have or need one. Incorrect pronunciation just sounds dreadful and the brand value that leaps to mind is unintelligent – to put it politely.

Chapter Six
The Future

Now What?

Congratulations for getting to the end of the book, or to the point at which you're ready to turn knowledge into action. At the beginning I said that what you know isn't as useful as what you do with what you know. I invite you to write actions that are SMART (specific, measurable, achievable, relevant and timely), in the personal brand action plan at the back of this book. Commit to doing them and don't forget to put the review dates in whatever type of personal organising system you use. Action without review is actually pointless.

Don't feel obligated to complete all the sections just for the sake of it. Equally, don't kid yourself there is no action at all you need to take. Given that consistency is key to evolving the brand you want, that's unlikely for most, if not all of us. No matter how busy and demanding your lifestyle, your personal brand and your personal impact are worth the effort. If you can't make the effort with your brand (and therefore yourself), why should anyone else?

Your personal brand and your personal image are to be invested in, delighted by and celebrated. My hope is that you've learned something from the book and get what you need when you make the investment in your own development.

Have fun.

Personal Brand Feedback Audit

Positive	*Developmental*
Personal Image	Personal Image
Non-Verbal Behaviour	Non-Verbal Behaviour
Verbal Behaviour	Verbal Behaviour

The Areas I Need To Focus On Within This Book Are:

Personal Brand Action Plan

Personal Image Actions	Review date
Non-verbal Behaviour Actions	Review date
Verbal Behaviour Actions	Review date

For more information on how Sarah Brummitt
can help you or your organisation, please go to
www.sarahbrummitt.com